ATLASES OF THE WORLD

ATLAS OF
AUSTRALIA
AND THE PACIFIC

S. JOSHUA COMIRE, MALCOLM PORTER, and KEITH LYE

This edition published in 2010 by:

The Rosen Publishing Group, Inc.
29 East 21st Street
New York, NY 10010

Library of Congress Cataloging-in-Publication Data

Comire, S. Joshua
Atlas of Australia and the Pacific / S. Joshua Comire,
    Malcolm Porter, and Keith Lye.
    p. cm. – (Atlases of the world)
Includes index.

ISBN 978-1-4358-8456-4 (library binding)
ISBN 978-1-4358-9113-5 (pbk.)
ISBN 978-1-4358-9119-7 (6-pack)

1. Australia–Maps. 2. New Zealand–Maps.
    3. Oceania–Maps. I. Porter, Malcolm. II. Lye, Keith.
    III. Rosen Central (Firm) IV. Title.

G2750.C6 2010
912.9–dc22

                                        2009582101

Manufactured in China

This edition published under license from
Cherrytree Books.

CPSIA Compliance Information: Batch #EW0102YA: For Further Information
contact Rosen Publishing, New York, New York at 1-800-237-9932

ATLASES OF THE WORLD
ATLAS OF AUSTRALIA
AND THE PACIFIC

This illustrated atlas combines maps, pictures, flags, globes, information panels, diagrams and charts to give an overview of the region and a closer look at each of its countries or states.

COUNTRY CLOSE-UPS

Each double-page spread has these features:

Introduction The author introduces the most important facts about the country, state or region.

Globe A globe on which you can see the country's or state's position in the continent and the world.

Flags Every country or state flag is shown.

Information panels Every country has an information panel that gives its area, population and capital, and where possible its other main towns, languages, religions, government and currency.

Pictures Important features of each country or state are illustrated and captioned to give a flavor of the country. You can find out about physical features, famous people, ordinary people, animals, plants, places, products, and much more.

Maps Every country or state is shown on a clear, accurate map. To get the most from the maps it helps to know the symbols that are shown in the key on the opposite page.

Land You can see by the coloring on the map where the land is forested, frozen or desert.

Height Relief hill shading shows where the mountain ranges are. Individual mountains are marked by a triangle.

Direction All of the maps are drawn with north at the top of the page.

Scale All of the maps are drawn to scale so that you can find the distance between places in miles or kilometers.

KEY TO MAPS

FIJI	Country name
Arnhem Land	Region
〜〜〜	Country border
- - - -	Country border at sea
▪	More than 1 million people*
•	More than 500,000 people
·	Less than 500,000 people
☐	Country capital
★	State capital
SOUTHERN ALPS	Mountain range
▲ Cook 15,771ft (4,807m)	Mountain with its height

Murray	River
⬭	Lake
- - - -	Seasonal river
⬭	Seasonal lake
⬭	Island

	Forest
	Crops
	Dry grassland
	Desert
	Tundra
	Polar

Population figures in all cases are estimates, based on the most recent censuses where available or a variety of other sources.

CONTINENT CLOSE-UPS

People and Beliefs Maps of population densities; chart of percentage of population by country; chart of areas of countries; map and chart of religions.

Climate and Vegetation Map of vegetation from mountain to desert; chart of land use; maps of winter and summer temperatures; map of annual rainfall.

Ecology and Environment Map of environmental damage to land and sea; panel on vanishing islands; panel and map of natural hazards; panels on environmental damage and endangered species.

Economy Maps of agricultural and industrial products; chart of gross domestic product for individual countries; panel on per capita gross domestic products; map of sources of energy.

Politics and History Panel of great events; maps of exploration of Australia and the Pacific; timeline of important dates.

CONTENTS

AUSTRALIA AND THE PACIFIC 4

COUNTRY CLOSE-UPS

AUSTRALIA 6
WESTERN AUSTRALIA 8
NORTHERN TERRITORY 10
SOUTH AUSTRALIA 12
QUEENSLAND 14
NEW SOUTH WALES 16
VICTORIA 18
TASMANIA 20

NEW ZEALAND 22
NORTH ISLAND 24
SOUTH ISLAND 26

PACIFIC OCEAN 28
MELANESIA 30
MICRONESIA 32
POLYNESIA 34

CONTINENT CLOSE-UPS

PEOPLE AND BELIEFS 36
CLIMATE AND VEGETATION 38
ECOLOGY AND ENVIRONMENT 40
ECONOMY 42
POLITICS AND HISTORY 44

GLOSSARY 46
FOR MORE INFORMATION 46
FOR FURTHER READING 46
INDEX 47

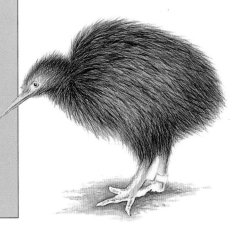

Kiwi
see page 22

AUSTRALIA AND THE PACIFIC

Australia, New Zealand, Papua New Guinea and the many, mostly small, islands scattered across the Pacific Ocean form a region called Oceania. This region does not include islands of eastern Asia, such as those that make up Indonesia, Japan and the Philippines.

Although Oceania extends over a vast area, it makes up less than 6 percent of the world's land area and contains only about 0.5 percent of the world's population. Oceania is dominated by Australia, which makes up 90 percent of the region. Australia is surrounded by water, but people do not regard it as an island. Instead, it is considered to be the world's smallest continent.

Arafura Sea

Exploration Captain James Cook (1728-79) was a British explorer who led three expeditions to the Pacific Ocean. He was the first European to visit the east coast of Australia, which he claimed for England, and many Pacific islands, including Hawaii (now a state of the United States).

AUSTRALIA

Cities About 85 percent of the people of Australia and New Zealand live in cities and towns. Many people work in factories or in services, such as government, finance or trade. However, both countries have important farming industries. This city is Melbourne, seen from one of its spacious suburbs.

INDIAN OCEAN

Marsupials Kangaroos are marsupials, mammals whose young are born in an immature state and reared in a pouch. With the exception of a few species, marsupials live only in Australia.

AUSTRALIA AND THE PACIFIC
Area: 3,283,946sq miles (8,505,380sq km)
Population: 33,000,000
Number of independent countries: 14

PAPUA NEW GUINEA

PACIFIC OCEAN

▲ *Wilhelm 793ft (4,509m)*

PACIFIC OCEAN

SOLOMON ISLANDS

Coral Sea

VANUATU

1 **MICRONESIA, FED. STATES OF**
2 **FIJI**
3 **KIRIBATI**
4 **NAURU**
5 **PALAU**
6 **MARSHALL ISLANDS**
7 **SAMOA**
8 **TONGA**
9 **TUVALU**

NEW CALEDONIA (France)

PACIFIC OCEAN

| 0 | | 500 miles |
| 0 | | 500 kilometers |

Tasman Sea

NEW ZEALAND

Geysers are hot springs that throw up columns of hot water and steam. Geysers can be seen in the volcanic region on North Island, New Zealand. Many islands in Oceania are volcanoes.

People The first people of Australia came from Southeast Asia and settled there more than 40,000 years ago. Today only about 400,000 of their descendants remain. Most of the population are descendants of more recent immigrants from Europe and Asia. These people are from Vietnam in Southeast Asia.

AUSTRALIA

Australia, which is officially called the Commonwealth of Australia, is the world's sixth largest country. Dutch navigators explored parts of its coast in the early 17th century. But European settlement began only in 1788 after the British Captain James Cook had explored the east coast. He named the whole of eastern Australia New South Wales.

European settlement was slow at first, but speeded up following gold rushes in the 1850s and 1890s. Most of these settlers came from Britain or Ireland, though after 1945 Australia admitted settlers from Eastern Europe. Since the 1970s, other immigrants have come from Southeast Asia, but Australia still retains many ties with Britain through the Commonwealth.

AUSTRALIA

Area: 2,966,153sq miles (7,682,300sq km)
Highest point: Mt Kosciuszko in the Australian Alps (part of the Great Dividing Range) 7,310ft (2,228m)
Population: 20,852,000
Capital: Canberra (pop 373,000)
Largest cities: Sydney (4,099,000)
Melbourne (3,447,000)
Brisbane (1,626,000)
Perth (1,376,000)
Adelaide (1,104,000)
Official language: English
Religions: Christianity (67%)
Government: Federal democracy (officially, constitutional monarchy)
Currency: Australian dollar

INDIAN OCEAN

Broome

Darwin

NORTHER

Dampier

Great Sandy Desert

Gibson Desert

Uluru
2,844ft (8

WESTERN AUSTRALIA

Great Victoria Desert

Kalgoorlie-Boulder

Perth
Fremantle

Great Australian Bight

Koalas are marsupials. They are sometimes called koala bears, but they are not related to bears. Koalas have sharp claws, long toes and a strong grip. They spend most of their lives in trees.

Boating and other watersports are popular on Australia's coasts. But exposure to the sun is dangerous, so most Australians now make sure their skin is protected.

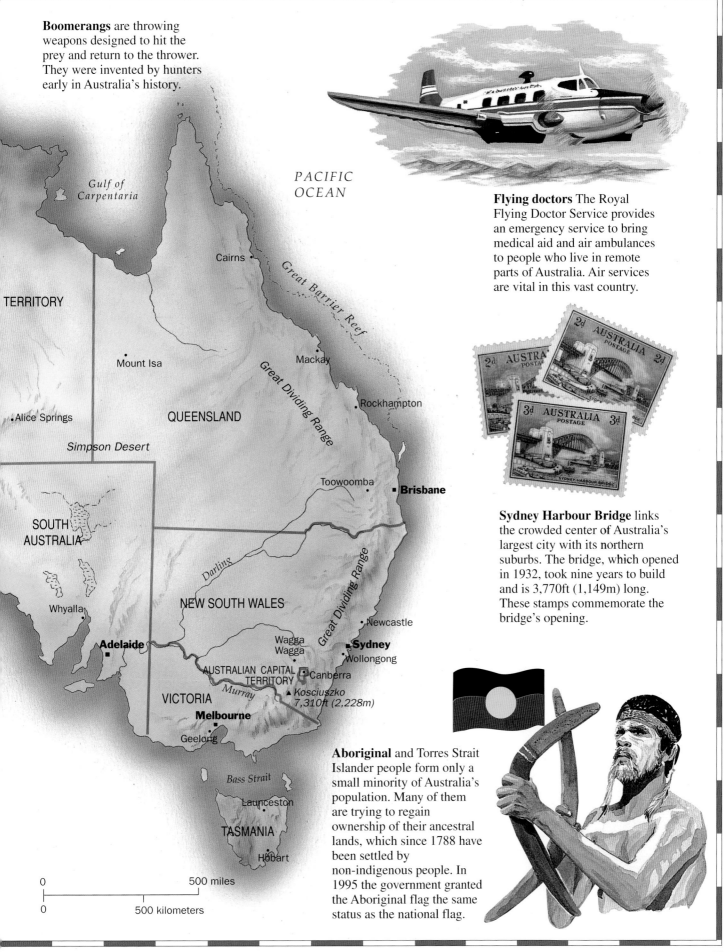

Boomerangs are throwing weapons designed to hit the prey and return to the thrower. They were invented by hunters early in Australia's history.

PACIFIC OCEAN

Flying doctors The Royal Flying Doctor Service provides an emergency service to bring medical aid and air ambulances to people who live in remote parts of Australia. Air services are vital in this vast country.

Sydney Harbour Bridge links the crowded center of Australia's largest city with its northern suburbs. The bridge, which opened in 1932, took nine years to build and is 3,770ft (1,149m) long. These stamps commemorate the bridge's opening.

Aboriginal and Torres Strait Islander people form only a small minority of Australia's population. Many of them are trying to regain ownership of their ancestral lands, which since 1788 have been settled by non-indigenous people. In 1995 the government granted the Aboriginal flag the same status as the national flag.

Gulf of Carpentaria

TERRITORY

Cairns

Great Barrier Reef

Mount Isa

Mackay

Great Dividing Range

Alice Springs

QUEENSLAND

Rockhampton

Simpson Desert

SOUTH AUSTRALIA

Toowoomba

■ **Brisbane**

Darling

Whyalla

NEW SOUTH WALES

Great Dividing Range

Newcastle

Wagga Wagga

Sydney

Adelaide

Wollongong

AUSTRALIAN CAPITAL TERRITORY

Canberra

Murray

VICTORIA

▲ *Kosciuszko* 7,310ft (2,228m)

Melbourne

Geelong

Bass Strait

Launceston

TASMANIA

Hobart

| 0 | | 500 miles |
| 0 | | 500 kilometers |

WESTERN AUSTRALIA

Australia consists of six states and two territories. The largest state, Western Australia, makes up nearly a third of the country, though it has only a tenth of its population. Much of the state is desert, but the north has hot, rainy summers and dry winters, and the southwest has dry summers and mild, rainy winters.

Minerals produced in Western Australia, including bauxite (aluminium ore), gold, iron ore, nickel and oil, have helped to make Australia prosperous. Agriculture, including dairy farming, is also important in the southwest. Major crops include fruit and wheat, while sheep are raised in dry areas.

Pearls and mother-of-pearl, the lining of the oyster shells in which pearls form, were obtained from Shark Bay, Western Australia, as early as 1850. In recent years, Australian and Japanese companies have set up pearl farms in both Western Australia and Queensland.

WESTERN AUSTRALIA

Area: 974,908sq miles (2,525,000sq km)
Highest point: Mount Meharry 4,104ft (1,251m)
Population: 2,081,000
Capital and largest city: Perth (pop 1,376,000)
Other large urban areas: Mandurah (85,000)
Kalgoorlie-Boulder (39,000)
Bunbury (27,000)
Floral emblem: Red and green kangaroo paw
Animal emblem: Numbat
Bird emblem: Black swan

Gold and diamonds Most of Australia's gold comes from Western Australia. Rich diamond fields were also discovered in the state in the 1970s. The Argyle mine in the Kimberley region is the world's largest diamond producer.

Pinnacles Desert, on the coast north of Perth, consists of a forest of thin peaks made of limestone. This area is part of the Nambung National Park. Australia has set up many national parks to protect its natural wonders and wildlife.

INDIAN OCEAN

Dampier · Port Hedland
Karratha
Marble Bar
Onslow
Hamersley Range
Ashburton
Meharry
4,104ft (1,251m)
Gascoyne
Carnarvon
Shark Bay
Murchison
Geraldton
INDIAN OCEAN

Northam
Perth ★
Fremantle
Mandurah
Bunbury
Swan
Katanning
Manjimup
Albany

Indian Ocean

The Indian Ocean extends from India in the north to Antarctica in the south. It washes the shores of western and southern Australia as far as the west coast of Tasmania. The east coast of Tasmania faces the Pacific Ocean.

Area: about 29,000,000sq miles (74,000,000sq km)
Average depth: 12,600ft (3,840m)
Deepest point: 25,344ft (7,725m)

ASIA
AFRICA
Java Trench
25,344ft (7,725m)
INDIAN OCEAN
AUSTRALIA
ANTARCTICA

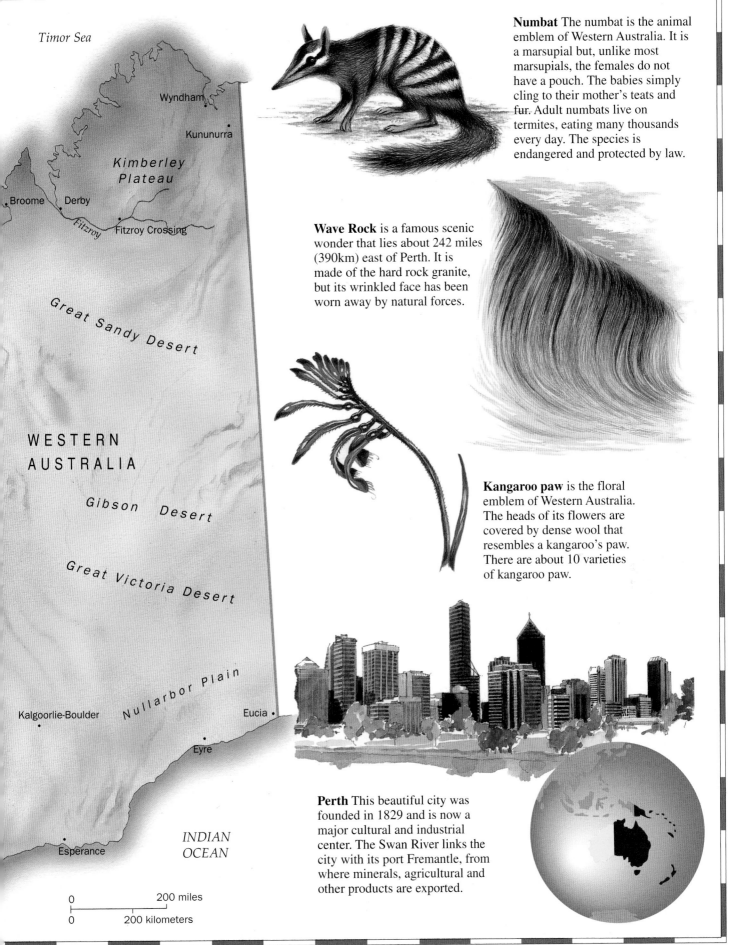

Timor Sea

Wyndham

Kununurra

Kimberley Plateau

Broome Derby

Fitzroy

Fitzroy Crossing

Great Sandy Desert

WESTERN AUSTRALIA

Gibson Desert

Great Victoria Desert

Kalgoorlie-Boulder

Nullarbor Plain

Eucia

Eyre

Esperance

INDIAN OCEAN

0   200 miles

0   200 kilometers

Numbat The numbat is the animal emblem of Western Australia. It is a marsupial but, unlike most marsupials, the females do not have a pouch. The babies simply cling to their mother's teats and fur. Adult numbats live on termites, eating many thousands every day. The species is endangered and protected by law.

Wave Rock is a famous scenic wonder that lies about 242 miles (390km) east of Perth. It is made of the hard rock granite, but its wrinkled face has been worn away by natural forces.

Kangaroo paw is the floral emblem of Western Australia. The heads of its flowers are covered by dense wool that resembles a kangaroo's paw. There are about 10 varieties of kangaroo paw.

Perth This beautiful city was founded in 1829 and is now a major cultural and industrial center. The Swan River links the city with its port Fremantle, from where minerals, agricultural and other products are exported.

NORTHERN TERRITORY

By far the largest of Australia's two territories is Northern Territory. The region has been mainly self-governing since 1978. Nearly a quarter of its people are Aboriginal and the territory contains many sacred Aboriginal sites, including the famous Uluru (Ayers Rock).

Northern Territory covers nearly a sixth of Australia, but it is the most thinly populated part of the country. The tropical north has a hot, rainy climate, but the south is mainly desert. Northern Territory is known for its fine scenery and its mineral deposits, which are its greatest source of wealth. Its minerals include bauxite, manganese, oil, natural gas and uranium.

NORTHERN TERRITORY

Area: 519,771sq miles (1,346,200sq km)
Highest point: Mount Zeil 4,954ft (1,510m)
Population: 213,000
Capital and largest city: Darwin (pop 94,000)
Other large urban areas: Alice Springs (26,000)
Floral emblem: Sturt's desert rose
Animal emblem: Red kangaroo
Bird emblem: Wedge-tailed eagle

Matthew Flinders (1774-1814), a British navigator, sailed around Australia between 1801 and 1803. He mapped much of the coastline and proved that there was no strait cutting through Australia, as some people thought.

Aboriginal art In ancient times, Aboriginal artists painted on cave walls and on bark. Many paintings were religious, while others depicted traditional ways of life.

Sturt's desert rose, the floral emblem of Northern Territory, is named after the explorer Charles Sturt. Its seven petals, which are shown on the territory's flag, symbolize the six states of Australia and Northern Territory.

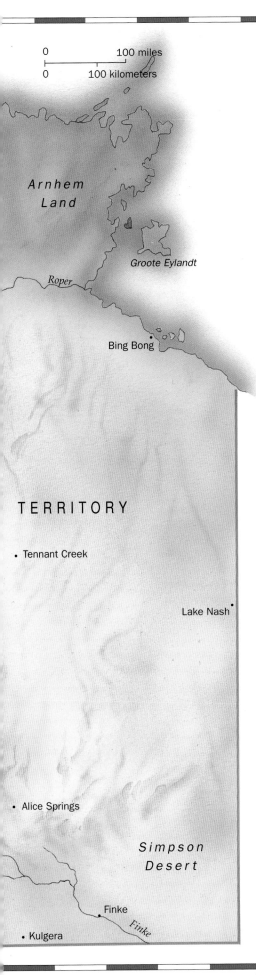

0   100 miles

0   100 kilometers

Arnhem Land

Groote Eylandt

Roper

Bing Bong

TERRITORY

• Tennant Creek

Lake Nash

• Alice Springs

Simpson Desert

Finke

• Kulgera

Finke

Darwin, capital of Northern Territory, is small, but it is a major communications center. The harbor on which it stands was named after the naturalist Charles Darwin in 1839. The first settlement on the harbor was not built until 1869.

Crocodiles Two types of crocodile live in the tropical lands in northern Australia. Saltwater crocodiles live in river mouths where tides bring in salt water. Freshwater crocodiles live in inland streams and lakes. Both species are protected though they are probably no longer endangered.

Uluru is an Aboriginal word meaning "great pebble." It is the Aboriginal name for a huge, red rock outcrop, formerly known as Ayers Rock, in the southern part of Northern Territory. Uluru is a major tourist attraction.

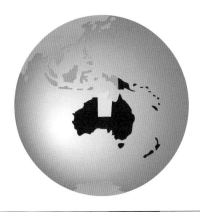

Kakadu National Park, which lies east of Darwin, is a World Heritage Site. About a third of Australia's bird species are seen there. It is especially well known for its waterbirds. The park also contains the world's largest and best preserved body of rock art.

SOUTH AUSTRALIA

South Australia is the third largest Australian state. About four-fifths of the land is desert and much of the land is covered by sand, or gibber, the local name for stony desert. The map of South Australia shows several lakes, including lakes Eyre and Gairdner. But these lakes only contain water after occasional storms. For most of the time, they are dry and covered by salt.

Most South Australians live in the southeast, which has hot, dry summers and mild, moist winters. This is a region of rich farmland, where barley, grapes (for wine-making) and wheat are grown. Sheep and cattle are also raised on the lush grazing land.

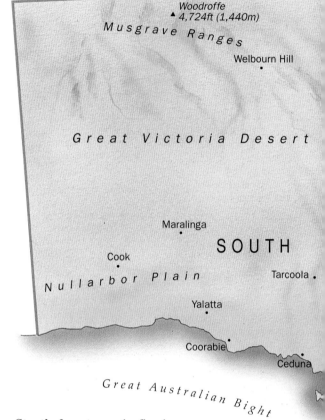

Woodroffe
▲ 4,724ft (1,440m)
Musgrave Ranges
Welbourn Hill
Great Victoria Desert
Maralinga
Cook
SOUTH
Tarcoola
Nullarbor Plain
Yalatta
Coorabie
Ceduna
Great Australian Bight

SOUTH AUSTRALIA

Area: 379,925sq miles (984,000sq km)
Highest point: Mount Woodroffe 4,724ft (1,440m)
Population: 1,576,000
Capital and largest city: Adelaide (pop 1,104,000)
Other large urban areas: Mount Gambier (23,000)
Whyalla (19,000)
Gawler (16,000)
Port Augusta (12,000)
Floral emblem: Sturt's desert pea
Animal emblem: Hairy-nosed wombat
Bird emblem: Piping shrike

Sturt's desert pea, the floral emblem of South Australia, is named after the explorer Charles Sturt. Large numbers of these plants, with their deep red flowers, bloom over vast areas after occasional rains. The plants produce hard, narrow brown pods, each containing many seeds that lie dormant until the next downpour.

Opals Australia is the world's leading producer of opal, a beautiful gemstone. The country's chief center of opal production is Coober Pedy, South Australia. It lies about 435 miles (700km) northwest of Adelaide.

Road trains are used to transport goods over huge distances in Australia. One high-powered truck pulls three or four large trailers along routes such as the Stuart Highway from Adelaide to Perth, which is 1,926 miles (3,100km) long.

Simpson Desert

Oodnadatta

Lake Eyre

Coober Pedy

AUSTRALIA · Marree

Woomera

Lake Everard

Lake Torrens

Lake Gairdner

Flinders Ranges

Lake Frome

Quorn

Port Augusta

Peterborough

Wudinna

Lock Whyalla Port Pirie

Wallaroo

Spencer Gulf

Gawler

Murray

Adelaide ★

Port Lincoln Warooka

Murray Bridge

Kingscote

Tailem Bend

Victor Harbor

Kangaroo Island

Millicent

Mount Gambier

```
0                    100 miles
0                    100 kilometers
```

Salt pans are huge dried-up "lakes" with a surface of salt. Because they are flat, they have often been used for car speed trials. In 1964 British driver, Donald Campbell, set a speed record for Class A land vehicles of 403.1mph (648.7km/h) at Lake Eyre Salt Flats, which was surpassed only in 2001.

Wheat is grown principally in a broad arc from southeastern South Australia, through Victoria and New South Wales into southeastern Queensland. Another wheat-growing area is in Western Australia.

Adelaide, South Australia's capital, is a major port, with a wide range of industries. The first colonists arrived in 1836. This carefully planned city is known for its many churches and the scenic coastlands and hills that surround it.

Kangaroo Island, South Australia, is Australia's third largest island. It was named after its large kangaroo population. The island has a sanctuary for the Australian fur seal on the south coast of Sea Bay. Its other attractions include fairy penguins and its scenic coastline.

QUEENSLAND

Queensland, the second largest state of Australia, has a warm climate and is often called the "Sunshine State." Off its coast lies the Great Barrier Reef, the world's largest coral formation. The Great Barrier Reef and the state's coastal resorts attract many tourists. The chief resort area is Gold Coast, south of Brisbane. This area extends along the coast into New South Wales.

The state is a major producer of sugar cane, while beef, dairy cattle and sheep are also important. Queensland has coal, copper and lead deposits, and manufacturing is a leading activity, especially in Brisbane.

 QUEENSLAND

Area: 666,798sq miles (1,727,000sq km)
Highest point: Mount Bartle Frere 5,285ft (1,611m)
Population: 4,132,000
Capital and largest city: Brisbane (pop 1,626,000)
Other large urban areas: Gold Coast (546,000)
Sunshine Coast (354,000)
Cairns (168,000)
Townsville (143,000)
Toowoomba (95,000)
Mackay (80,000)
Floral emblem: Cooktown orchid
Animal emblem: Koala
Bird emblem: Brolga

Pineapples are grown in Queensland. Bananas also thrive in the tropical conditions. In cooler areas, temperate fruits, such as apples, are grown. The most valuable crops are grains, including barley, corn, sorghum and wheat.

Torres Strait

Cape York
Bamaga
Weipa
Lockhart River
Cape York Peninsula
Gulf of Carpentaria
Mitchell
Mornington
Karumba
Burketown
Normanton
Mt Surprise
Saxby
Mount Isa
Cloncurry
Hughender
QUEENSLAND
Winton
Longreach
Great Artesian Basin
Birdsville

Mount Isa in western Queensland has some of the world's richest mines. Deposits of copper, lead, silver and zinc, which are found close together, are all mined at Mount Isa. Queensland is also a leading coal producer.

Cattle ranching is Queensland's most valuable farming activity. The main ranching area is in east-central Queensland. Dairy farming is important in the southeast, especially around Brisbane.

Great Barrier Reef This reef of coral extends about 1,250 miles (2,010km) along the coast of Queensland. Parts of the reef lie about 10 miles (16km) from the coast. Other parts lie more than 100 miles (160km) from the mainland. Many islands are scattered throughout the reef.

PACIFIC OCEAN

Surfing is one of the many outdoor sports at which Australians excel. The southern coasts of Queensland contain popular surfing points. Skin diving, swimming and boating are also popular pastimes.

Brisbane, the capital of Queensland, stands on the Brisbane River, which flows into the Pacific Ocean. It is a busy river port and a prosperous trading and manufacturing center. It was founded in 1824 as a settlement for convicts.

0   100 miles

0   100 kilometers

Cooktown

Port Douglas

Mareeba • Cairns

Gordonvale

Innisfail

Bartle Frere
5,285ft (1,611m)

Great Barrier Reef

Ingham

Townsville

Bowen

Charters Towers

Proserpine

Belyando

Mackay

Sarina

Great Dividing Range

Dawson

Rockhampton

Mount Morgan

Gladstone

Bundaberg

Maryborough

Fraser

Charleville

Miles

Roma

Sunshine Coast

Toowoomba

★ **Brisbane**

Ipswich

Cunnamulla

Southport

Gold Coast

Goondiwindi

Coolangatta

Mungindi

NEW SOUTH WALES

New South Wales is the richest and most developed Australian state. Although it ranks fourth in area, it contains more people than any other state. The cities of Sydney, Newcastle and Wollongong contain about three-quarters of the state's people. New South Wales was originally the name for a British colony that covered the whole of eastern Australia. It assumed roughly its present borders in 1863.

Enclosed in the southeastern corner of New South Wales is the small Australian Capital Territory. This area was chosen as the site of Australia's federal capital, Canberra, in 1909.

NEW SOUTH WALES

Area: 309,500sq miles (801,600sq km)
Highest point: Mount Kosciuszko 7,310ft (2,228m)
Population: 6,855,000
Capital and largest city: Sydney (pop 4,099,000)
Other large urban areas: Newcastle (502,000)
Wollongong (263,000)
Albury (114,000)
Floral emblem: Waratah
Animal emblem: Platypus
Bird emblem: Kookaburra

AUSTRALIAN CAPITAL TERRITORY

Area: 927sq miles (2,400sq km)
Population: 336,000

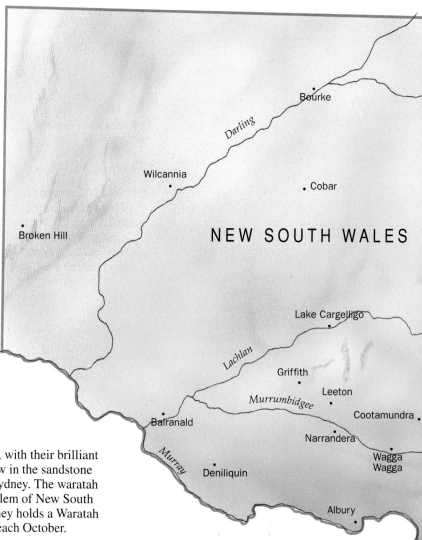

Waratah plants, with their brilliant red flowers, grow in the sandstone region around Sydney. The waratah is the floral emblem of New South Wales, and Sydney holds a Waratah Spring Festival each October.

Canberra, in Australian Capital Territory, is the national capital, where the parliament, consisting of the Senate and House of Representatives, meets. The layout of this handsome city was originally planned by an American architect, Walter Burley Griffin.

Washing machines are among many products made in New South Wales, which is Australia's top manufacturing state. Others include cars, chemicals, clothing, farm implements, fertilizers, glassware, iron and steel, machinery, paper and textiles.

Blue Mountains These scenic mountains west of Sydney are part of the Great Dividing Range. Once they formed a daunting barrier to settlers and stopped them reaching the interior plains. But a road was built through the mountains in 1815.

Platypus The platypus is often called a duckbill, because it has a bill like a duck's. It is one of only two kinds of mammals that lay eggs, the other being the echidna. Both live only in Australia.

Sydney Opera House stands on a peninsula that juts into Sydney Harbour. Its sail-like roofs, made of overlapping shells, give it an unforgettable appearance. It was opened in 1973.

Kosciuszko National Park, in southeastern New South Wales, is a major tourist and ski resort. It lies in the Australian Alps, part of the Great Dividing Range. Among its beautiful snowy mountains and lakes is Mount Kosciuszko, Australia's highest peak.

Byron Bay
Yetman
Lismore
Tenterfield
Walgett
Grafton
Armidale
Coffs Harbour
Kempsey
Tamworth
Port Macquarie
Dubbo
Taree
Forster
Muswellbrook
Mudgee
Parkes
Maitland
Orange
Newcastle
Cowra
The Entrance
Gosford
Young
Sydney
★
Yass
Campbelltown
Wollongong
Goulburn
Kiama
Canberra
Nowra
AUSTRALIAN CAPITAL TERRITORY
Cooma
Eden

Great Dividing Range

0   100 miles
0   100 kilometers

VICTORIA

Victoria is the smallest of Australia's mainland states. Yet, with about 50 people to every square mile (20 per sq km), it is the most densely populated part of the country. Victoria has a higher proportion of people from non-English-speaking countries than any other state. It contains sizeable communities of Italian, Greek and Vietnamese people.

Victoria has large areas of fertile land. Farming is important, but the state's prosperity now depends mainly on industry. Victoria produces brown coal, oil and natural gas, together with a wide range of manufactured products.

VICTORIA

Area: 87,877sq miles (227,600sq km)
Highest point: Mount Bogong 6,516ft (1,986m)
Population: 5,165,000
Capital and largest city: Melbourne (pop 3,447,000)
Other large urban areas: Geelong (152,000)
Ballarat (86,000)
Bendigo (83,000)
Floral emblem: Pink heath
Animal emblem: Leadbeater's possum
Bird emblem: Helmeted honeyeater

Australian Rules football is a fast, exciting form of football, invented by Australians and played only in Australia and Papua New Guinea. Other popular team sports include cricket, rugby league, rugby union and soccer.

Grapes are grown in Victoria. Some are dried and exported as currants, raisins and sultanas. Others are used to make wine. Top-quality Australian wines are enjoyed around the world.

Mildura

Murray

Ouyen

Swan Hill

Kerang

Echuca

Nhill

Warracknabeal

VICTORIA

Dimboola

Horsham

Bendigo

Stawell

St Arnaud

Castlemaine

Daylesford

Ararat

Ballarat

Bacchus Marsh

Geelong

Portland

Warrnambool

Colac

Lorne

Twelve Apostles is the name of a series of limestone stacks along the southwest coast of Victoria. Stacks are fragments of the coast that have been cut off from the shore by the continuous battering of sea waves.

Sheep More than two-fifths of Victoria's farmland is used to raise sheep. Victoria is a major exporter of lamb, live sheep and wool. Beef and dairy products are also important, and major crops include wheat and other grains, hay and potatoes.

Murray River This river rises in the Snowy Mountains and is Australia's longest permanently flowing river. It is used to produce hydroelectricity and also to irrigate the land. Visitors take pleasure trips on its paddle steamers.

Ned Kelly (1855-80) was the best known of Australia's bushrangers, or outlaws. He was born in Victoria. He and members of his gang made armor to protect their bodies from gunfire. Many poor people regarded him as a hero.

Melbourne is Australia's second largest city after Sydney. It contains about three-quarters of Victoria's population. It was founded on the Yarra River at the head of Port Phillip Bay in 1835. It is now a major commercial, financial and industrial center.

Rochester

Shepparton

Murray

Wodonga

Benalla

Wangaratta

Snowy Mts

Bogong
6,516ft (1,986m)

Euroa

G r e a t   D i v i d i n g   R a n g e

Melbourne
★

Port Phillip Bay

Orbost

Bairnsdale

Traralgon

Sale

Yarram

Wonthaggi

B a s s   S t r a i t

0   100 miles

0   100 kilometers

TASMANIA

Tasmania, Australia's smallest state, is cut off from mainland Australia by the 149-mile (240-km) wide Bass Strait. The island was discovered by the Dutch navigator Abel Tasman in 1642. He named it Van Diemen's Land, after the governor of the Dutch East Indies, but the British renamed it Tasmania in 1855.

Tasmania is mountainous with a rainy, temperate climate. Its resources include valuable minerals, forests and rivers that are used to produce hydroelectricity. Farmers raise cattle and sheep and grow crops such as apples and potatoes.

TASMANIA

Area: 26,178sq miles (67,800sq km)
Highest point: Mount Ossa 5,305ft (1,617m)
Population: 492,000
Capital: Hobart (pop 208,000)
Other large urban areas: Launceston (74,000)
Burnie (20,000)
Devonport (19,000)
Floral emblem: Tasmanian blue gum
Animal emblem (unofficial): Tasmanian devil
Bird emblem (unofficial): Green rosella parrot

Hydroelectric dams have been built on many of Tasmania's rivers to take advantage of the heavy rainfall that swells the fast-flowing rivers. The electricity powers industries that manufacture refined metals, including zinc, iron ore, copper and tin, wood and paper products, and processed farm products.

Abel Tasman (1603-59), a Dutch navigator, sailed all the way round Australia in 1642 but never sighted the mainland. But he did visit Tasmania, which is named after him. On a second voyage in 1644, he explored parts of the northern and western coasts of Australia.

INDIAN OCEAN

Tasmanian blue gum
This beautiful eucalyptus tree is the state's floral emblem. Forests cover nearly half of Tasmania, with beech and myrtle being common in the wettest areas and eucalypts in areas with rainfall of 30-59in (76-150cm).

Apples Tasmania was once called the "Apple Isle," but apples ceased to be a major crop after the state lost its British markets in the 1970s, when Britain became part of the European Economic Community (now the European Union, or EU). British membership of the EU has weakened ties between Australia and Britain.

Tasmanian devil This fierce marsupial, up to a 39in (1m) long including its tail, feeds on animals, living or dead. It lives only on Tasmania though once it also lived on the Australian mainland. The Tasmanian wolf, another marsupial native to the island, is now thought to be extinct.

Hobart, the capital of Tasmania, is an important port on the estuary of the Derwent River. The city was founded in 1804 as a port and whaling center. Industries in the city now produce cement, wood pulp and metal products.

Hobart Cup The Sydney-Hobart yacht race covers 630 nautical miles (1,134km). It starts on December 26 each year and the fastest yachts cover the distance in little over three days. The first race was held in 1945.

Palana

Flinders

Cape Barren

Bass Strait

Tasman Sea

Devonport

George Town

Gladstone

Launceston

St Marys

Great Lake

Ross

Bronte

Swansea

Coles Bay

TASMANIA

Hamilton

Lake Gordon

Dunalley

Glenorchy

Hobart ★

Bruny

```
0                    50 miles
|____|____|____|____|____|
0                    50 kilometers
```

NEW ZEALAND

New Zealand is a remote country, lying about 994 miles (1,600km) southeast of Australia. Its first people were the Maori, who came to Aotearoa, their name for New Zealand, from islands to the northeast more than 1,200 years ago. The first European to reach the islands was the Dutch navigator Abel Tasman in 1642.

The Dutch did not settle, however, and in 1769, Captain James Cook rediscovered New Zealand and charted the coasts of the main islands. This led Britons to settle from 1814. Today most New Zealanders are of British or other European descent. About six percent are of Asian origin. Eight percent are Maori and almost as many part-Maori. In addition, almost 180,000 are descendants of Pacific Islanders.

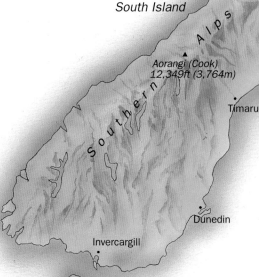

Sheep farming is important in New Zealand, where there are more sheep than people. Major products include butter, cheese, meat, especially lamb and venison, and wool. But manufacturing is now the country's most valuable activity. Processed foods are the chief manufactures.

NEW ZEALAND

Area: 104,454sq miles (270,534sq km)
Highest point: Aorangi (Mount Cook), in the Southern Alps, 12,349ft (3,764m)
Population: 4,076,000
Capital: Wellington (pop 343,000)
Largest cities: Auckland (953,000)
Hamilton (158,000)
Hastings and Napier (120,000)
Dunedin (116,000)
Palmerston North (76,000)
Official language: English
Religions: Christianity (60%)
Government: Parliamentary democracy (officially, constitutional monarchy)
Currency: New Zealand dollar

Kiwi fruit are grown in New Zealand, especially in the area around the Bay of Plenty on North Island. Kiwi fruit, which were called Chinese gooseberries until the New Zealanders renamed them, are exported to many countries.

Tasman Sea

South Island

Aorangi (Cook)
12,349ft (3,764m)

Timaru

Dunedin

Invercargill

Stewart Island

Kiwis are flightless birds that live only in New Zealand. They are seldom seen because they come out only at night. They live in forests and forage for worms and insects on the ground.

War chants The Maori are famous for their *haka*, or war chants. These are shouted in a rhythmic way by Maori warriors – and rugby teams. One well-known chant, *Ka-mate, ka-mate*, is supposed to have been composed by a famous chief named Te Rauparaha.

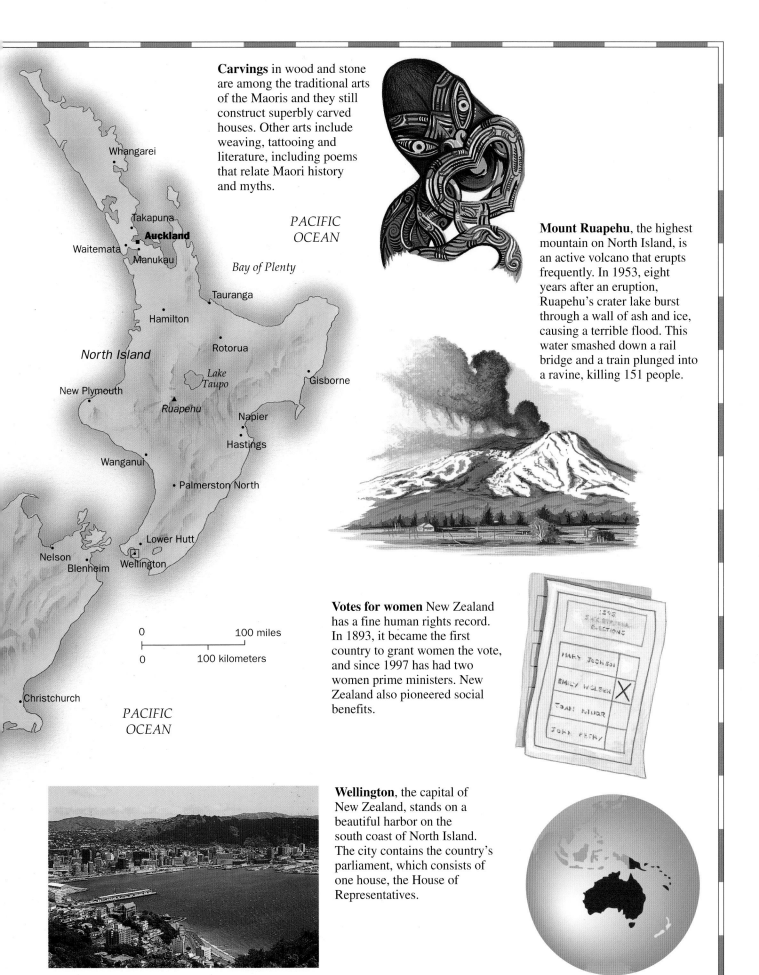

Carvings in wood and stone are among the traditional arts of the Maoris and they still construct superbly carved houses. Other arts include weaving, tattooing and literature, including poems that relate Maori history and myths.

Whangarei

Takapuna

Auckland

Waitemata

Manukau

PACIFIC OCEAN

Bay of Plenty

Tauranga

Hamilton

North Island

Rotorua

Lake Taupo

New Plymouth

Gisborne

Ruapehu

Napier

Hastings

Wanganui

Palmerston North

Lower Hutt

Nelson

Blenheim

Wellington

0   100 miles

0   100 kilometers

Christchurch

PACIFIC OCEAN

Mount Ruapehu, the highest mountain on North Island, is an active volcano that erupts frequently. In 1953, eight years after an eruption, Ruapehu's crater lake burst through a wall of ash and ice, causing a terrible flood. This water smashed down a rail bridge and a train plunged into a ravine, killing 151 people.

Votes for women New Zealand has a fine human rights record. In 1893, it became the first country to grant women the vote, and since 1997 has had two women prime ministers. New Zealand also pioneered social benefits.

Wellington, the capital of New Zealand, stands on a beautiful harbor on the south coast of North Island. The city contains the country's parliament, which consists of one house, the House of Representatives.

NORTH ISLAND

North Island is New Zealand's second largest island. It contains hilly regions in the south, a central volcanic region and, in the north, peninsulas that jut into the Pacific Ocean. The volcanic region contains three active volcanoes: Mount Ruapehu, the highest, Mount Ngauruhoe and Mount Tongariro. There are also many hot springs and geysers. Much of North Island was formed by volcanic activity within the last four million years.

North Island contains Wellington, the country's capital, and Auckland, the largest city and chief manufacturing center.

0 _____ 50 miles
0 _____ 50 kilometers

Tasman Sea

Auckland is the largest city in New Zealand. It has grown rapidly as more and more people have been attracted by its semi-tropical climate and casual lifestyle. Most work in the city center and live in sprawling suburbs connected by many motorways.

Dairy farming is a major activity on North Island, where most of the country's nine million cattle are raised. Butter and cheese are the leading dairy products on the island and are among New Zealand's leading exports. Dried milk is also exported. Northern North Island has a warm climate, and subtropical crops, such as avocados and citrus fruits, are grown there.

Mount Egmont is a dormant (sleeping) volcano that last erupted more than 300 years ago. A Maori legend tells how a lover's quarrel between Egmont (Taranaki in Maori) and Mount Tongariro explains its isolated position in the southwestern part of North Island.

North Cape

Whangarei

Dargaville

Hauraki Gulf

East Coast Bays

Takapuna

Auckland
Mount Roskill · Papatoeto
Waitemata
Manukau · Papakura

Hamilton

New Plymouth

Egmont
8,261ft (2,518m)

Wanganui

Wanganui

Palmerston North

Upper Hutt

Porirua

Lower Hutt

Cook Strait

Wellington

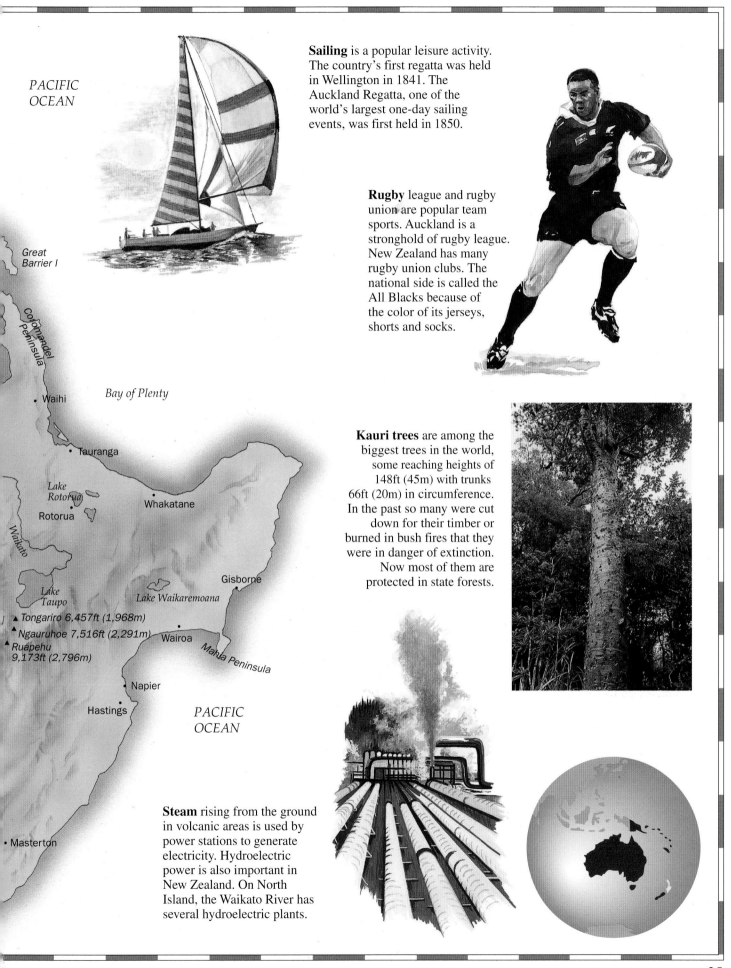

PACIFIC
OCEAN

Sailing is a popular leisure activity. The country's first regatta was held in Wellington in 1841. The Auckland Regatta, one of the world's largest one-day sailing events, was first held in 1850.

Rugby league and rugby union are popular team sports. Auckland is a stronghold of rugby league. New Zealand has many rugby union clubs. The national side is called the All Blacks because of the color of its jerseys, shorts and socks.

Great
Barrier I

Coromandel
Peninsula

Waihi

Bay of Plenty

Tauranga

Lake
Rotorua

Whakatane

Rotorua

Waikato

Gisborne

Lake
Taupo

Lake Waikaremoana

▲ Tongariro 6,457ft (1,968m)
▲ Ngauruhoe 7,516ft (2,291m)
▲ Ruapehu
9,173ft (2,796m)

Wairoa

Mahia Peninsula

Kauri trees are among the biggest trees in the world, some reaching heights of 148ft (45m) with trunks 66ft (20m) in circumference. In the past so many were cut down for their timber or burned in bush fires that they were in danger of extinction. Now most of them are protected in state forests.

Napier

Hastings

PACIFIC
OCEAN

Masterton

Steam rising from the ground in volcanic areas is used by power stations to generate electricity. Hydroelectric power is also important in New Zealand. On North Island, the Waikato River has several hydroelectric plants.

SOUTH ISLAND

The Southern Alps on South Island contain the country's highest peak, Aorangi (Aoraki), which means "cloud piercer" in Maori, and is also known as Mount Cook. Rivers of ice called glaciers fill high mountain valleys. Long ago, the glaciers flowed down to sea level, carving out deep valleys, which are now sea inlets called fiords.

On the east-central coast of South Island lie the Canterbury Plains, a major grain-growing region. Livestock farming is important in the southeast. The country's third largest island, Stewart Island, lies off the south coast of South Island.

Grapes grow well on South Island and there are many vineyards producing wine for export. Other important crops include apples, barley, pears, potatoes and other vegetables, and wheat.

0   50 miles
0   50 kilometers

Southern Alps This young mountain range, which forms the backbone of South Island, was pushed up from the ocean floor in the last 10 to 15 million years. Evergreen forests swathe its slopes. At higher levels there are glaciers and ice fields.

Milford Sound is one of many fiords in the southwest coastal area of Fiordland. It is the only fiord that can be reached by road. The whole coast is ragged with steep-sided inlets with hundreds of waterfalls and magnificent scenery.

Tasman Sea

Westland Bight

Southern Alps

Aorangi (Cook)
12,349ft (3,764m)

Lake Tekapo

Lake Pukaki

Lake Benmore

Waitaki

Milford Sound

Lake Hawea

Lake Wanaka

Queenstown

Lake Wakatipu

Lake Te Anau

Dunedin

Gore

Clutha

Invercargill

Foveaux Strait

Stewart Island

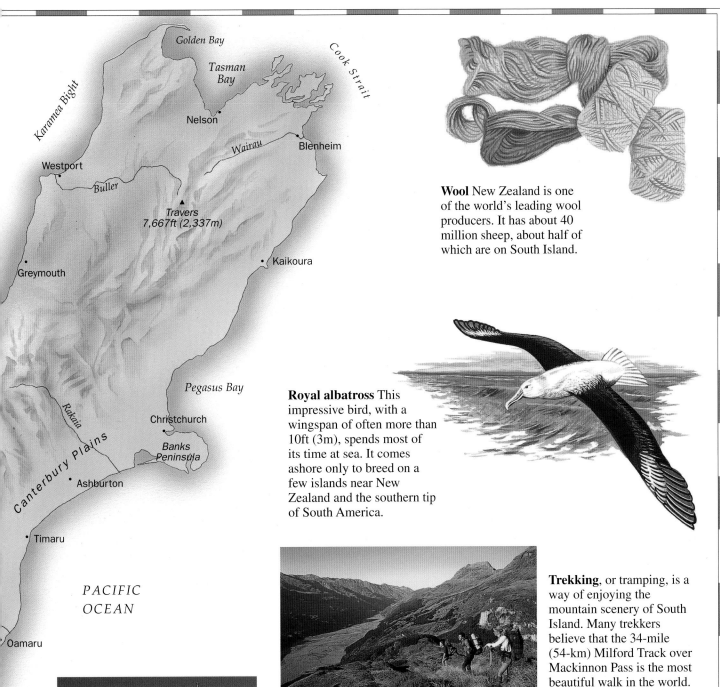

Golden Bay

Tasman Bay

Cook Strait

Karamea Bight

Nelson

Wairau

Blenheim

Westport

Buller

Travers
7,667ft (2,337m)

Greymouth

Kaikoura

Pegasus Bay

Rakaia

Christchurch

Canterbury Plains

Banks Peninsula

Ashburton

Timaru

PACIFIC
OCEAN

Oamaru

Wool New Zealand is one of the world's leading wool producers. It has about 40 million sheep, about half of which are on South Island.

Royal albatross This impressive bird, with a wingspan of often more than 10ft (3m), spends most of its time at sea. It comes ashore only to breed on a few islands near New Zealand and the southern tip of South America.

Trekking, or tramping, is a way of enjoying the mountain scenery of South Island. Many trekkers believe that the 34-mile (54-km) Milford Track over Mackinnon Pass is the most beautiful walk in the world. Tourism is growing in importance in New Zealand.

Christchurch, the largest city on South Island, lies on the edge of the Canterbury Plains, one of New Zealand's leading wheat-growing and sheep-raising regions. Many of the city's industries process farm products. Christchurch was founded in 1851. This is a view of the cathedral.

PACIFIC OCEAN

The Pacific is the largest and deepest of the world's four oceans. It covers about a third of the world's surface. It stretches from the Bering Strait, which links it to the icy Arctic Ocean in the north, to Antarctica in the south. The Pacific is widest near the equator. Between mainland Malaysia and Panama, it is about 15,000 miles (24,000km) wide.

The Pacific contains many islands. Some of the islands are high and mountainous, others low and flat. The mountainous islands are active or dormant volcanoes that rise from the ocean floor. Other islands are low-lying, rising only a few meters above sea level. These are made of coral. The Pacific islands are divided into three geographical and cultural groups: Melanesia, Micronesia and Polynesia.

PACIFIC OCEAN
Area: 69,884,500sq miles (181,000,000sq km)
Average depth: 12,900ft (3,940m)
Deepest point: Mariana Trench 36,198ft (11,033m)

International Date Line
This imaginary line roughly corresponds to the 180° line of longitude, which runs through the Pacific. Because time is measured east and west of Greenwich (0°) at a rate of one hour per 15 degrees, there is a difference of 24 hours at the 180° line of longitude. Travellers from west to east gain a day as they cross the line, those going east-west lose one.

Whales can be seen off many Pacific coasts. These great mammals divide their time between warm seas where they give birth and cold seas where feeding is good. The blue whale, which is the largest animal that has ever lived, is found in all oceans, but whaling has made it scarce.

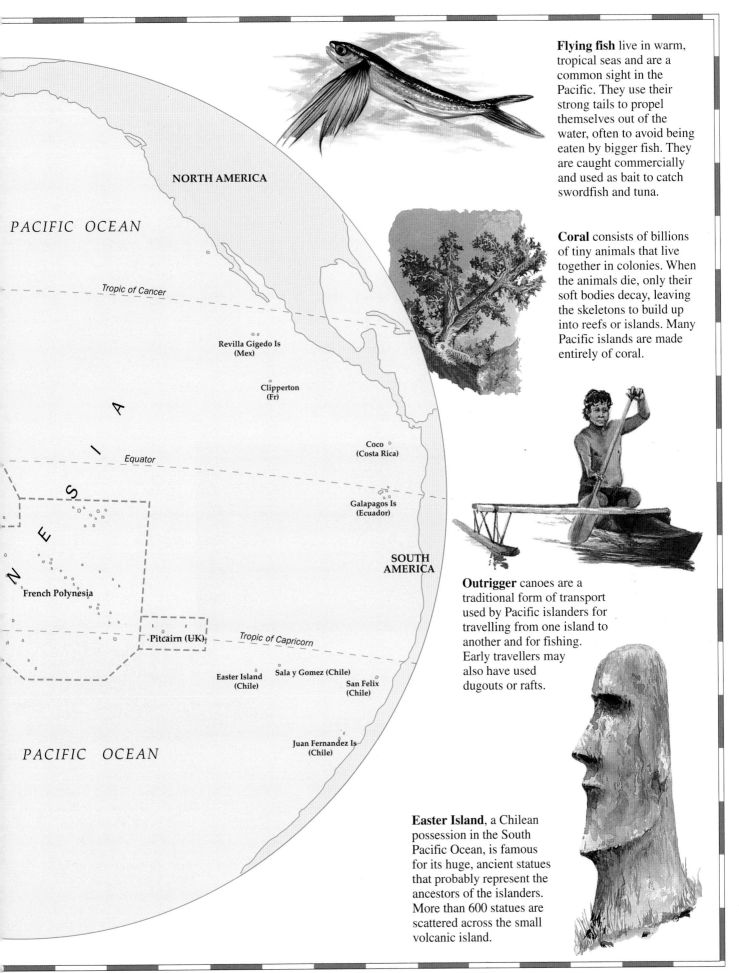

Flying fish live in warm, tropical seas and are a common sight in the Pacific. They use their strong tails to propel themselves out of the water, often to avoid being eaten by bigger fish. They are caught commercially and used as bait to catch swordfish and tuna.

Coral consists of billions of tiny animals that live together in colonies. When the animals die, only their soft bodies decay, leaving the skeletons to build up into reefs or islands. Many Pacific islands are made entirely of coral.

Outrigger canoes are a traditional form of transport used by Pacific islanders for travelling from one island to another and for fishing. Early travellers may also have used dugouts or rafts.

Easter Island, a Chilean possession in the South Pacific Ocean, is famous for its huge, ancient statues that probably represent the ancestors of the islanders. More than 600 statues are scattered across the small volcanic island.

NORTH AMERICA

PACIFIC OCEAN

Tropic of Cancer

Revilla Gigedo Is
(Mex)

Clipperton
(Fr)

Coco
(Costa Rica)

Equator

Galapagos Is
(Ecuador)

SOUTH
AMERICA

French Polynesia

Pitcairn (UK)

Tropic of Capricorn

Easter Island
(Chile)

Sala y Gomez (Chile)

San Felix
(Chile)

Juan Fernandez Is
(Chile)

PACIFIC OCEAN

MELANESIA

Melanesia includes four independent countries and two territories. Papua New Guinea is by far the largest country in the region. It consists of the eastern part of the island of New Guinea, while the western part belongs to Indonesia, a country in Asia. The other three independent countries in Melanesia are, in order of size, Solomon Islands, Fiji and Vanuatu. Vanuatu was formerly ruled jointly by Britain and France and called New Hebrides.

Volcanoes are common on the islands of Papua New Guinea, and many are active. These volcanoes form part of an unstable part of the earth called the Pacific "ring of fire."

PAPUA NEW GUINEA

Madang

Wilhelm ▲
14,793ft (4,509m) • Lae

New Britain

Gulf of Papua

Port Moresby

PAPUA NEW GUINEA

Area: 178,704sq miles (462,840sq km)
Highest point: Mt Wilhelm 14,793ft (4,509m)
Population: 5,671,000
Capital and largest city: Port Moresby (pop 275,000)
Languages: Melanesian pidgin, Molu, English, many local languages
Religions: Christianity (Protestant 44%, Roman Catholic 22%), traditional beliefs
Government: Constitutional monarchy
Currency: Kina

FIJI

Area: 7,056sq miles (18,274sq km)
Highest point: Mt Tomanivi, on Viti Levu, 4,341ft (1,323m)
Population: 906,000
Capital and largest city: Suva (pop 210,000)
Languages: English, Fijian, Hindustani
Religions: Christianity (52%), Hinduism (38%), Islam (8%)
Government: Republic
Currency: Fijian dollar

Tourism is important in Fiji and elsewhere in Melanesia because it provides jobs for local people. Many remote Pacific islands hold out hope for the development of the tourist industry.

SOLOMON ISLANDS

Area: 11,157sq miles (28,896sq km)
Highest point: Mt Makarakomburu 8,028ft (2,447m)
Population: 552,000
Capital and largest city: Honiara (pop 56,000)
Languages: Melanesian pidgin, English (official)
Religion: Christianity (97%)
Government: Constitutional monarchy
Currency: Solomon Islands dollar

VANUATU

Area: 4,706sq miles (12,189sq km)
Highest point: Mt Tabwemasana 6,165ft (1,879m)
Population: 209,000
Capital and largest city: Port-Vila (pop 34,000)
Languages: Bislama, English, French, many local languages
Religion: Christianity (72%)
Government: Republic
Currency: Vatu

Territories
New Caledonia (French overseas territory)
Norfolk Island (Australian territory), south of New Caledonia.

Mining is important in Papua New Guinea, which exports oil, copper, gold and other metals. One island, Bougainville, has a huge copper mine. The people there objected to the mining and fought a long civil war, which began in the late 1980s and continued until a peace agreement was signed in 1998.

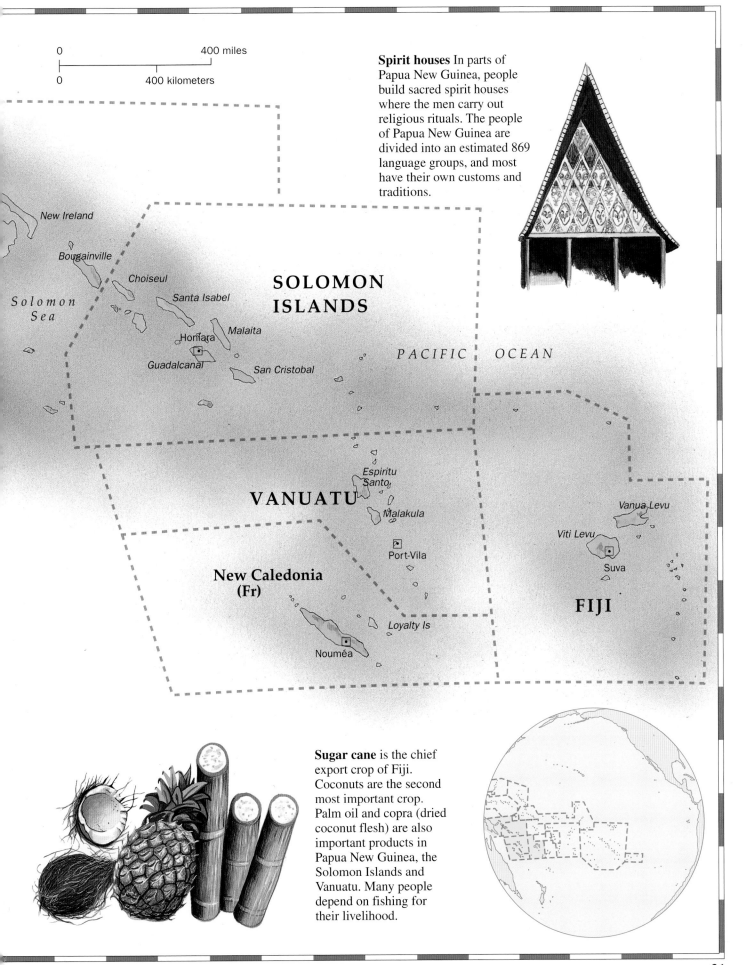

0   400 miles

0   400 kilometers

Spirit houses In parts of Papua New Guinea, people build sacred spirit houses where the men carry out religious rituals. The people of Papua New Guinea are divided into an estimated 869 language groups, and most have their own customs and traditions.

New Ireland

Bougainville

Choiseul

Solomon Sea

Santa Isabel

SOLOMON ISLANDS

Honiara

Malaita

Guadalcanal

San Cristobal

PACIFIC OCEAN

Espiritu Santo

VANUATU

Malakula

Vanua Levu

Viti Levu

Port-Vila

Suva

New Caledonia (Fr)

FIJI

Loyalty Is

Nouméa

Sugar cane is the chief export crop of Fiji. Coconuts are the second most important crop. Palm oil and copra (dried coconut flesh) are also important products in Papua New Guinea, the Solomon Islands and Vanuatu. Many people depend on fishing for their livelihood.

31

MICRONESIA

Micronesia includes the Pacific islands north of Melanesia, which number more than 2,000. Most of them are small, low-lying coral islands.

The largest country in Micronesia is the Republic of Kiribati (formerly the Gilbert Islands). It became independent in 1979. The Federated States of Micronesia and the Republic of the Marshall Islands are former United States territories. They became independent in 1991. The Republic of Palau, which became independent in 1994, is another former United States territory. The tiny Republic of Nauru became independent in 1968.

Sharks are common in the warm waters of the central Pacific. All sharks are meateaters and most of the 350 or so species are small and timid. Only a few big ones eat big fishes, and very few are big enough to attack people.

KIRIBATI

Area: 280sq miles (726sq km)
Highest point: 266ft (81m) on Banaba Island
Population: 105,000
Capital and largest city: Bairiki on Tarawa Atoll (pop 47,000)
Languages: Kiribati, English
Religion: Christianity
Government: Republic
Currency: Australian dollar

MARSHALL ISLANDS

Area: 70sq miles (181sq km)
Highest point: 33ft (10m) on Likiep
Population: 60,000
Capital and largest city: Majuro on Majuro Atoll (pop 28,000)
Languages: Marshallese, English
Religion: Christianity
Government: Republic
Currency: US dollar

MICRONESIA, FEDERATED STATES OF

Area: 271sq miles (702sq km)
Highest point: Totolom 2,595ft (791m)
Population: 108,000
Capital: Palikir on Pohnpei (pop 4,000)
Official language: English
Religion: Christianity
Government: Federal republic
Currency: US dollar

PALAU

Area: 177sq miles (459sq km)
Highest point: Mt Ngerchelchuus 794ft (242m)
Population: 17,000
Capital: Melekeok on Babelthuap (pop 390)
Largest city: Koror (pop 14,000)
Official languages: Palauan, English
Religion: Christianity
Government: Republic
Currency: US dollar

NAURU

Area: 8sq miles (21sq km)
Highest point: 200ft (61m)
Population: 13,000
Capital: Yaren (pop 5,000)
Official language: Nauruan
Religion: Christianity
Government: Republic
Currency: Australian dollar

Territories
Guam (US territory)
Northern Mariana Islands (US commonwealth)
Wake Island (US possession)

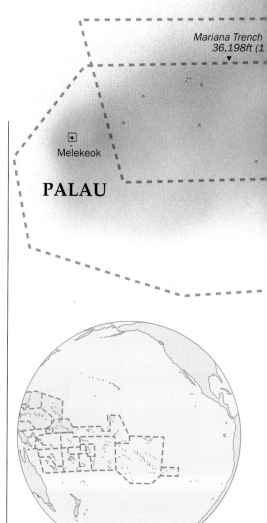

Mariana Trench
36,198ft (1

Melekeok

PALAU

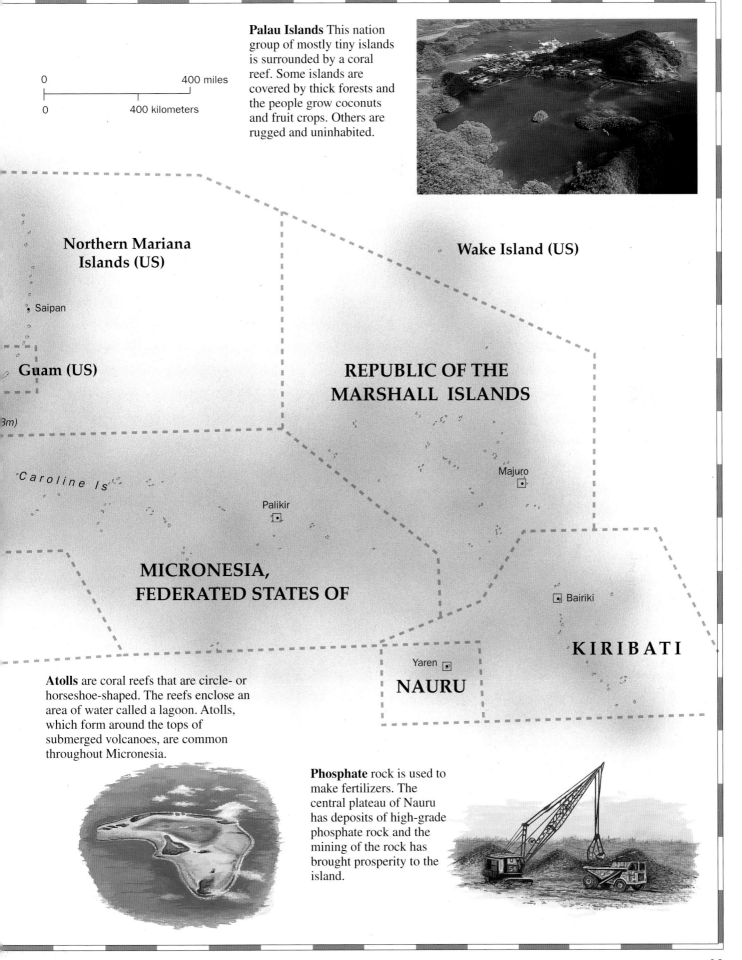

Palau Islands This nation group of mostly tiny islands is surrounded by a coral reef. Some islands are covered by thick forests and the people grow coconuts and fruit crops. Others are rugged and uninhabited.

0 _____ 400 miles

0 _____ 400 kilometers

Northern Mariana
Islands (US)

Wake Island (US)

Saipan

Guam (US)

REPUBLIC OF THE
MARSHALL ISLANDS

3m)

Caroline Is

Majuro

Palikir

MICRONESIA,
FEDERATED STATES OF

Bairiki

Yaren

KIRIBATI

NAURU

Atolls are coral reefs that are circle- or horseshoe-shaped. The reefs enclose an area of water called a lagoon. Atolls, which form around the tops of submerged volcanoes, are common throughout Micronesia.

Phosphate rock is used to make fertilizers. The central plateau of Nauru has deposits of high-grade phosphate rock and the mining of the rock has brought prosperity to the island.

POLYNESIA

Polynesia covers a vast area in the Pacific Ocean, between Midway Island in the north, New Zealand in the southwest, and Easter Island in the southeast.

This vast expanse of water contains three independent countries and several territories, listed below. The largest country is Samoa, which was formerly called Western Samoa. Samoa was once ruled by New Zealand, but it became fully independent in 1962. Tonga, which consists of more than 170 islands, was a British protectorate, but it became independent in 1970. Tuvalu, formerly the British Ellice Islands, became independent in 1978.

SAMOA

Area: 1,086sq miles (2,813sq km)
Highest point: Mauga Silisli 6,096ft (1,858m)
Population: 177,000
Capital and largest city: Apia (pop 40,000)
Official languages: Samoan, English
Religion: Christianity
Government: Constitutional monarchy
Currency: Tala

TONGA

Area: 288sq miles (747sq km)
Highest point: Mt Kao 3,389ft (1,033m)
Population: 115,000
Capital and largest city: Nuku'alofa (pop 35,000)
Official languages: Tongan, English
Religion: Christianity
Government: Constitutional monarchy
Currency: Pa'anga

TUVALU

Area: 10sq miles (26sq km)
Highest point: 15ft (4.6m) on Niulakita
Population: 12,000
Capital and largest city: Fongafale on Funafuti island (pop 6,000)
Official language: none
Religion: Christianity
Government: Constitutional monarchy
Currency: Tuvalu dollar

Sea turtles live throughout the Pacific Ocean. Females spend their lives in the sea, returning to the land only to lay their eggs. Most males never return to land after they enter the sea as hatchlings. Most species are endangered.

Shells As well as eating the contents of some of them, Pacific islanders use shells to make jewelry and ornaments for the tourist trade. Once shells were used as money, and today collectors still pay high prices for the rarest deep-water shells.

Territories

American Samoa (US territory)
Cook Islands (self-governing territory in association with New Zealand)
Easter Island (Chilean dependency)
French Polynesia (French overseas territory)
Midway Island (US possession)
Niue (New Zealand)
Pitcairn Islands Group (British overseas territory)
Tokelau (New Zealand territory)
Wallis & Futuna Islands (French overseas territory)

Hawaii (US State)

Midway Island (US)

Johnston Island (US)

Phoenix Is

TUVALU
Fongafale

Tokelau (NZ)

SAMOA
Apia

American Samoa (US)

Wallis & Futuna Islands (Fr)

TONGA
Nuku'alofa

Niue (NZ)

International Date Line

NEW ZEALAND

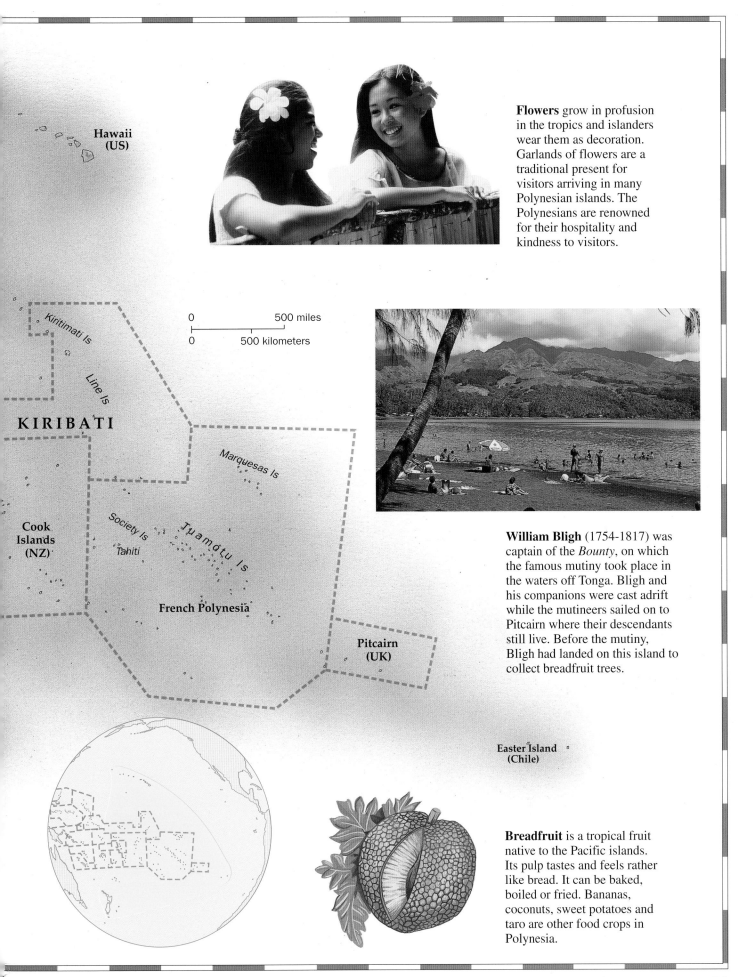

Flowers grow in profusion in the tropics and islanders wear them as decoration. Garlands of flowers are a traditional present for visitors arriving in many Polynesian islands. The Polynesians are renowned for their hospitality and kindness to visitors.

Hawaii
(US)

Kiritimati Is

Line Is

KIRIBATI

Marquesas Is

Cook
Islands
(NZ)

Society Is

Tahiti

Tuamotu Is

French Polynesia

Pitcairn
(UK)

Easter Island
(Chile)

William Bligh (1754-1817) was captain of the *Bounty*, on which the famous mutiny took place in the waters off Tonga. Bligh and his companions were cast adrift while the mutineers sailed on to Pitcairn where their descendants still live. Before the mutiny, Bligh had landed on this island to collect breadfruit trees.

Breadfruit is a tropical fruit native to the Pacific islands. Its pulp tastes and feels rather like bread. It can be baked, boiled or fried. Bananas, coconuts, sweet potatoes and taro are other food crops in Polynesia.

PEOPLE AND BELIEFS

Australia, New Zealand and the Pacific islands cover a vast area, but they contain only 0.5 percent of the world's population. Much of the region, including most of the interior of Australia, is thinly populated or empty of people. Most Australians live along the eastern, southeastern and southwestern coasts in large cities, notably Sydney, Melbourne, Brisbane, Adelaide and Perth. Much of Papua New Guinea is covered by thinly populated rainforests. New Zealand, with its fertile farmland and its many cities and towns, is the most densely populated of the three main countries in the region.

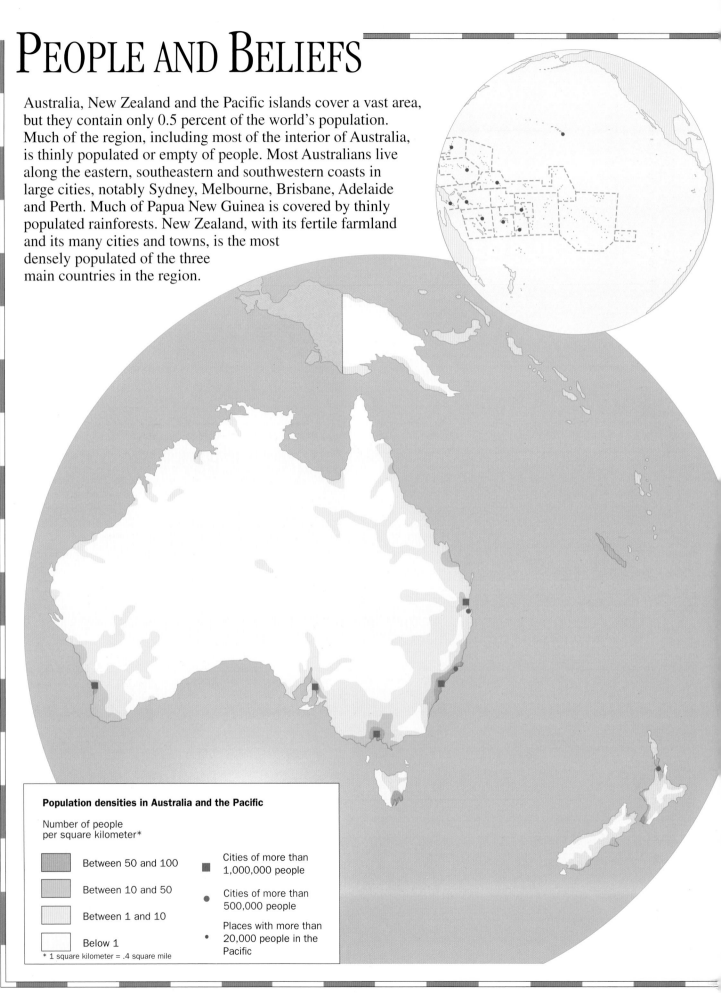

Population densities in Australia and the Pacific

Number of people
per square kilometer*

▨ Between 50 and 100	■ Cities of more than 1,000,000 people
▨ Between 10 and 50	● Cities of more than 500,000 people
▨ Between 1 and 10	• Places with more than 20,000 people in the Pacific
▢ Below 1	

* 1 square kilometer = .4 square mile

Population and area

Australia, the smallest of the world's seven continents, covers 91 percent of the land in the Pacific region. It also contains more than 60 percent of the total population. Papua New Guinea and New Zealand rank second and third in both area and population. Some of the small Pacific island nations, including Fiji, Samoa, Tonga and Tuvalu, are much more densely populated than the three largest countries.

Percentage of population of Australia and the Pacific by country

AUSTRALIA 63% PAPUA NEW GUINEA 18% NEW ZEALAND 13% FIJI 3% SOLOMON ISLANDS 2% ALL OTHER COUNTRIES 1%

Areas of countries within Australia and the Pacific

AUSTRALIA 91% PAPUA NEW GUINEA 5% NEW ZEALAND 3% ALL OTHER COUNTRIES 1%

Main religions

Before the arrival of European missionaries in the late 18th century, most people in Australia and the Pacific followed ancient religions based on a belief in spirits and numerous gods. The people told many stories about how the gods created the world and how they still interact with people during religious ceremonies.

For example, the Aboriginal people of Australia believed that the world was created by gods and goddesses during a period called the Dreaming. The spirits of these gods had merged with nature and could be contacted through rituals.

Christian missionaries worked hard to stamp out traditional beliefs and, today, most of the people are Christians. The religious beliefs of the people reflect their countries of origin. For example, people of Irish, French or Italian origin are usually members of the Roman Catholic Church, while people of English origin are generally Anglicans. Immigrants from Asia are mostly Muslims, Hindus or Buddhists.

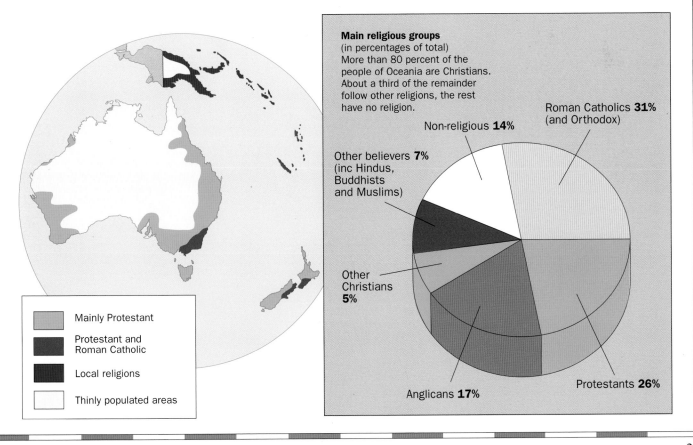

Mainly Protestant

Protestant and Roman Catholic

Local religions

Thinly populated areas

Main religious groups
(in percentages of total)
More than 80 percent of the people of Oceania are Christians. About a third of the remainder follow other religions, the rest have no religion.

Roman Catholics **31%** (and Orthodox)

Non-religious **14%**

Other believers **7%** (inc Hindus, Buddhists and Muslims)

Other Christians **5%**

Anglicans **17%**

Protestants **26%**

CLIMATE AND VEGETATION

Papua New Guinea, the Solomon Islands, Vanuatu and many other Pacific islands lie in the tropics. This region has a hot climate, often with heavy rainfall, and rainforests cover much of the land. The northern part of Australia also lies in the tropics. It has a hot, wet summer season (between November and April) and a hot, dry winter season (May to October). The interior of Australia is dry, containing deserts and dry grasslands. Southern Australia has four seasons with most of the rain falling in winter. New Zealand has a mild, rainy climate, although the mountains in South Island have cold, snowy winters. North Island has a warmer climate than South Island.

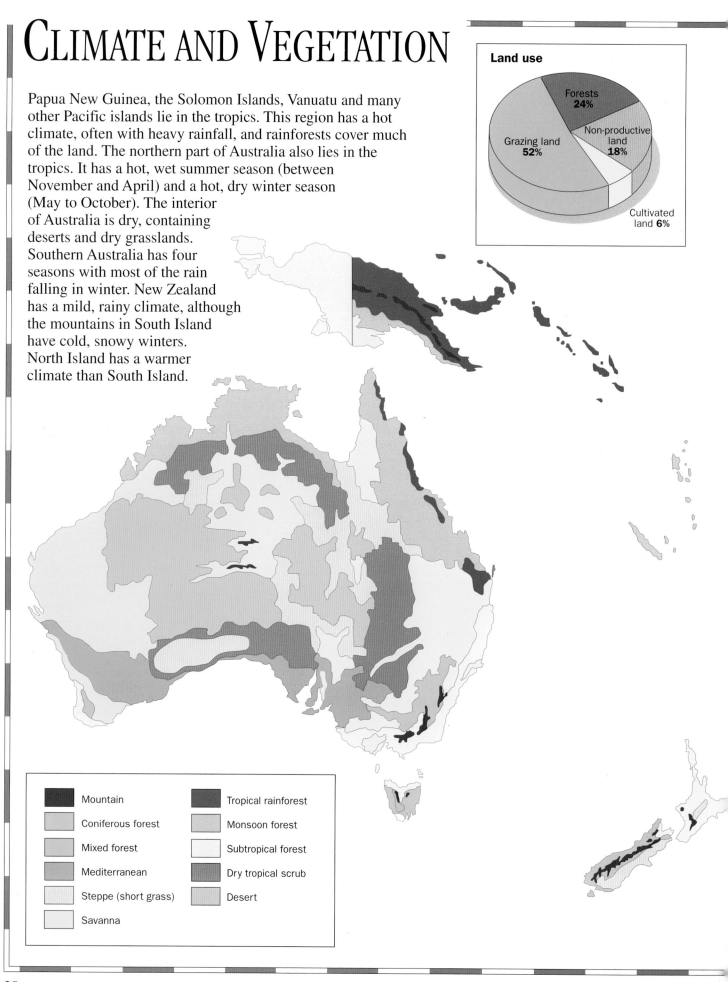

Land use

- Grazing land **52%**
- Forests **24%**
- Non-productive land **18%**
- Cultivated land **6%**

	Mountain		Tropical rainforest
	Coniferous forest		Monsoon forest
	Mixed forest		Subtropical forest
	Mediterranean		Dry tropical scrub
	Steppe (short grass)		Desert
	Savanna		

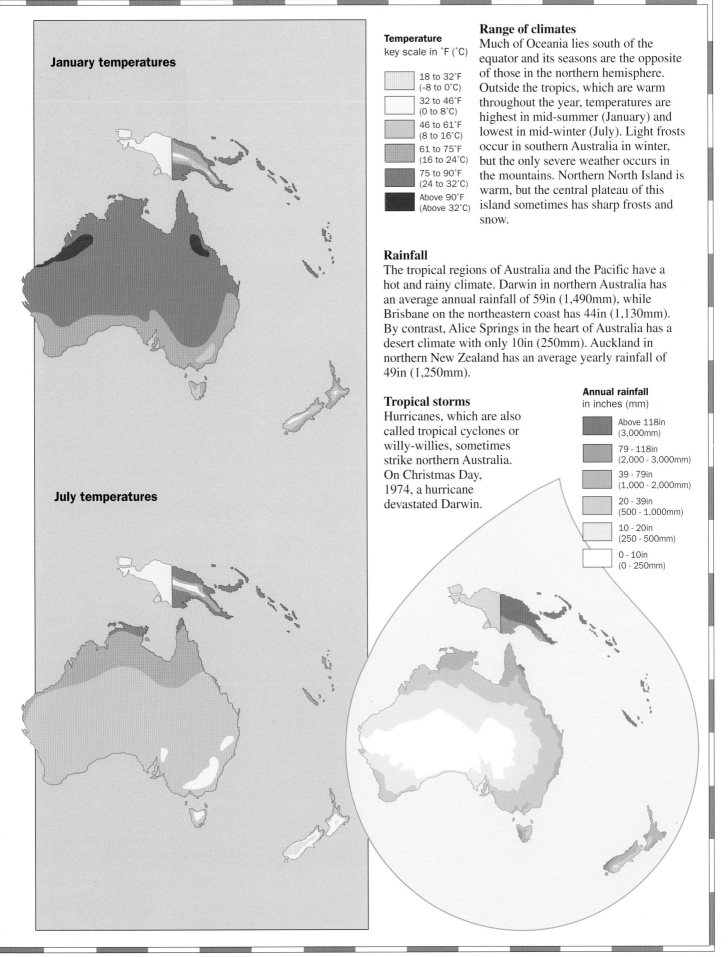

January temperatures

Temperature
key scale in ˚F (˚C)

18 to 32˚F
(–8 to 0˚C)

32 to 46˚F
(0 to 8˚C)

46 to 61˚F
(8 to 16˚C)

61 to 75˚F
(16 to 24˚C)

75 to 90˚F
(24 to 32˚C)

Above 90˚F
(Above 32˚C)

Range of climates

Much of Oceania lies south of the equator and its seasons are the opposite of those in the northern hemisphere. Outside the tropics, which are warm throughout the year, temperatures are highest in mid-summer (January) and lowest in mid-winter (July). Light frosts occur in southern Australia in winter, but the only severe weather occurs in the mountains. Northern North Island is warm, but the central plateau of this island sometimes has sharp frosts and snow.

Rainfall

The tropical regions of Australia and the Pacific have a hot and rainy climate. Darwin in northern Australia has an average annual rainfall of 59in (1,490mm), while Brisbane on the northeastern coast has 44in (1,130mm). By contrast, Alice Springs in the heart of Australia has a desert climate with only 10in (250mm). Auckland in northern New Zealand has an average yearly rainfall of 49in (1,250mm).

July temperatures

Tropical storms

Hurricanes, which are also called tropical cyclones or willy-willies, sometimes strike northern Australia. On Christmas Day, 1974, a hurricane devastated Darwin.

Annual rainfall
in inches (mm)

Above 118in
(3,000mm)

79 - 118in
(2,000 - 3,000mm)

39 - 79in
(1,000 - 2,000mm)

20 - 39in
(500 - 1,000mm)

10 - 20in
(250 - 500mm)

0 - 10in
(0 - 250mm)

ECOLOGY AND ENVIRONMENT

Around 200 million years ago, all of the world's continents were grouped together. But from 180 million years ago, the single, huge supercontinent broke up and Australia became isolated from the other land areas. As a result, its plants and animals evolved differently from those of other land masses. None of its native mammals gives birth to fully formed babies, like those in the rest of the world.

Early settlers modified the land through hunting and farming, but their effect was small compared with that of the Europeans. European settlement during the last two centuries badly damaged the fragile environments of Australia, New Zealand and other Pacific islands.

Nuclear tests After vigorous protests by pressure groups and governments, nuclear testing in the Pacific has stopped, but nobody knows how much long-term environmental damage it caused to the region.

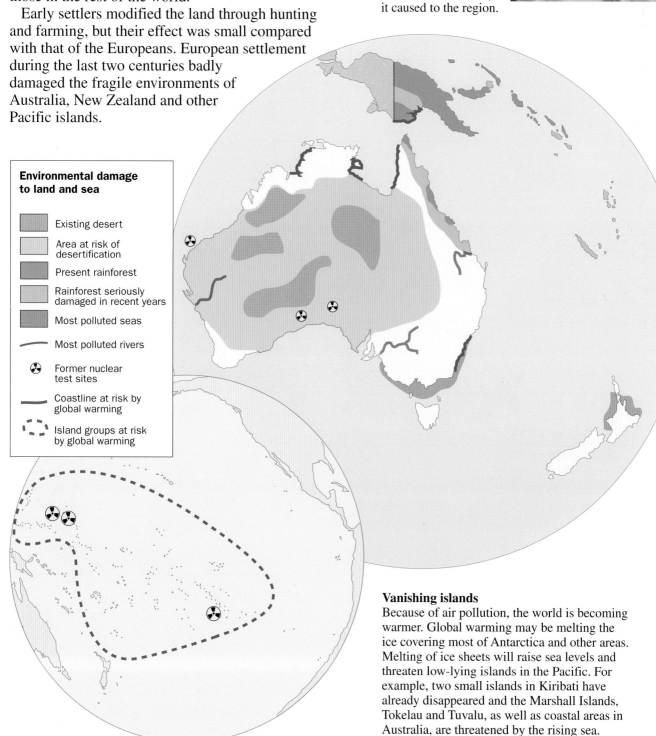

Environmental damage to land and sea

- Existing desert
- Area at risk of desertification
- Present rainforest
- Rainforest seriously damaged in recent years
- Most polluted seas
- —— Most polluted rivers
- ☢ Former nuclear test sites
- —— Coastline at risk by global warming
- ┄┄ Island groups at risk by global warming

Vanishing islands
Because of air pollution, the world is becoming warmer. Global warming may be melting the ice covering most of Antarctica and other areas. Melting of ice sheets will raise sea levels and threaten low-lying islands in the Pacific. For example, two small islands in Kiribati have already disappeared and the Marshall Islands, Tokelau and Tuvalu, as well as coastal areas in Australia, are threatened by the rising sea.

Damaging the environment

Farming methods brought from Europe have damaged the land. In dry areas, huge herds of cattle and sheep have stripped away the dry grasses and turned the land into desert. Forest clearance has led to a loss of three-quarters of Australia's tropical forest, while more than a third of the country's woodland has been cut down or severely damaged. This destruction has led to the extinctions of many animal species.

Settlers rashly introduced plants and animals from Europe. After rabbits were released into the wild, they stripped the land bare and helped turn grasslands into deserts. Other introduced animals, including foxes and domestic cats, preyed on indigenous animals and helped make them extinct.

One famous natural wonder, the Great Barrier Reef, is now threatened by pollution, fishing and global warming.

Radioactive contamination has also occurred in Australia and on some Pacific islands where nuclear weapons have been tested. Today many people are aware of the threat to the environment and are working to conserve the region's wildlife.

Natural hazards

Earthquakes and volcanoes occur in a zone running from Papua New Guinea, through the Solomon Islands to Vanuatu. Another zone stretches from Samoa to New Zealand. Other natural hazards include storms, droughts and bush fires. In 2006/7 Australia suffered its worst recorded drought.

The Great Barrier Reef, one of the world's richest ecosystems, is periodically threatened by the crown-of-thorns starfish, which attacks the coral. Scientists are still trying to find out why sudden explosions of the starfish population occur.

Natural hazards

- ▨ Earthquake zones
- ▲ Active volcanoes
- ◉ Areas affected by annual tropical cyclones (January - March)
- ✹ Recent droughts
- 🔥 Areas recently hit by major bush fires

Endangered species

Australia has a higher rate of extinction of mammals than any other continent in the world. One famous example is the Tasmanian wolf, which was hunted to extinction by farmers wanting to protect their livestock. In New Zealand, the moa, a flightless bird, was also hunted to extinction by Polynesian peoples. Many extinctions have occurred on the Pacific islands.

Today, conservation is an important issue. In Australia, the National Parks and Wildlife Service is seeking to halt the rate of extinctions that have marked the last 200 years, while New Zealand now protects most of its native species. In both countries, thousands of people have joined demonstrations against developments that may harm the environment.

Some endangered species

Birds
Akiapolaau (Hawaiian finch)
Australian ground parrot
Black stilt (NZ)
Kagu (New Caledonia)
Kakapo (NZ)
Short-tailed albatross (Pacific)

Mammals and reptiles
Brush-tailed rat kangaroo (Aus)
Leadbeater's possum (Aus)
Northern hairy-nosed wombat (Aus)
Numbat (Aus)
Tuatara (NZ)

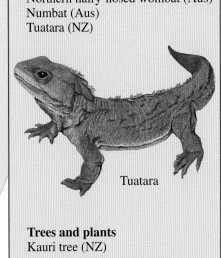

Tuatara

Trees and plants
Kauri tree (NZ)

ECONOMY

Australia and New Zealand are prosperous countries, but most of the Pacific islands are far less developed. Until about 50 years ago, the economy of the region was based on farming. Australia and New Zealand were major producers of dairy products, especially butter and cheese, lamb, sugar, wheat and wool. Enormous quantities of these goods were sold to the industrial countries of Europe.

Australia is also a major world producer of minerals. Today its mines yield minerals such as bauxite, coal, copper, diamonds, manganese, nickel, oil and natural gas, silver, tin, tungsten and zinc, which it exports to industrial countries in eastern Asia, including Japan. But manufacturing is now the most valuable activity in both Australia and New Zealand.

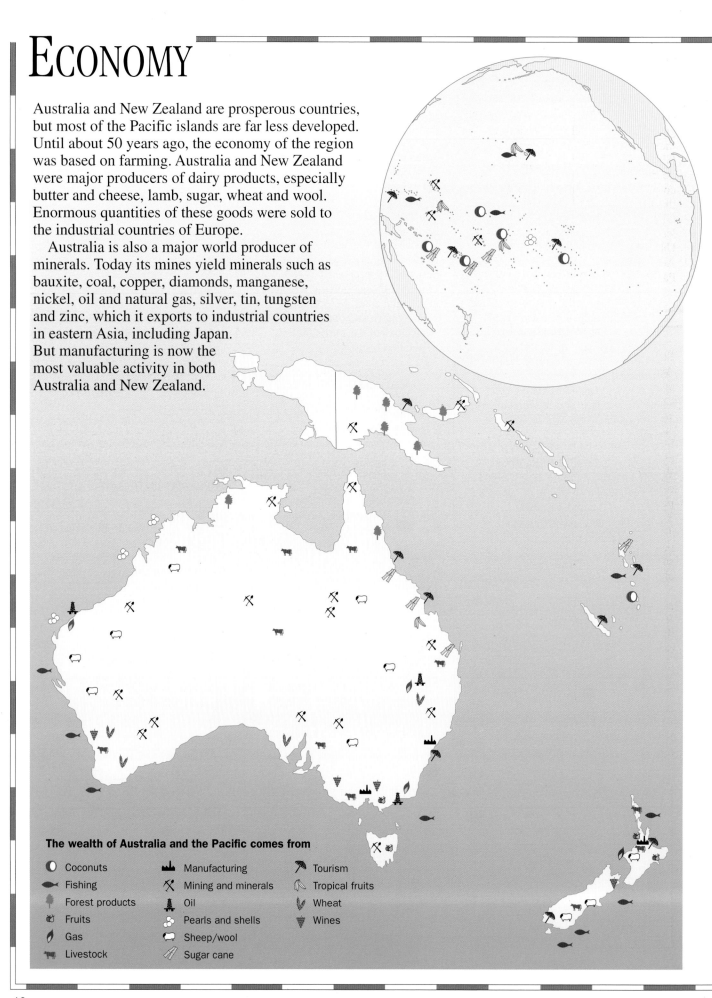

The wealth of Australia and the Pacific comes from

Coconuts	Manufacturing	Tourism
Fishing	Mining and minerals	Tropical fruits
Forest products	Oil	Wheat
Fruits	Pearls and shells	Wines
Gas	Sheep/wool	
Livestock	Sugar cane	

Gross domestic product

To compare the economies of countries, experts calculate the gross domestic product (GDP) of the countries in US dollars. The GDP is the total value of the goods and services produced by a country in a year. The chart shows that the country with the highest GDP is Australia. Its total GDP is less than one-twentieth that of the United States. Following Australia come New Zealand, Papua New Guinea and Fiji.

GDP for the countries of Australia and the Pacific (in billions of dollars)

Australia **(701)**

New Zealand **(109)**
Papua New Guinea **(5)**
All other countries **(5)**

Sources of energy

Australia has abundant energy-producing resources. Coal is the major source of energy and the main coalfields are in Queensland and New South Wales. Australia also exports coal. Victoria and Western Australia also produce oil and natural gas. Hydroelectric plants, especially those in the Snowy Mountains and in Tasmania, produce about 10 percent of Australia's energy supply. Solar energy plants are also being developed.

Hydroelectric plants, especially on the Waikato River on North Island and on the Clutha and Waitaki rivers on South Island, account for much of the electrical energy produced in New Zealand. Thermal energy is also obtained from volcanic steam on North Island. New Zealand also produces coal.

Per capita GDPs

Per capita means per head or per person. Per capita GDPs are worked out by dividing the GDP by the population. For example, the per capita GDP of Australia is US $34,577. By contrast, the Solomon Islands has a per capita GDP of only $518, which places it among the world's poorer countries.

Sources of energy found in Australia and the Pacific

- 🛢 Oil
- 💧 Gas
- ≈ Hydroelectricity
- ⚒ Coal
- ☢ Uranium

POLITICS AND HISTORY

Britain played a major part in the modern history of Australia and New Zealand. But after Britain joined the European Economic Community (now the European Union) in 1973, the ties with Britain were loosened, though both countries remain members of the Commonwealth and cultural relationships are strong. Since 1973, Australia and New Zealand have found new markets for their exports, with trading partners in eastern Asia and North America.

Another political issue is the status of the first people in the region, including the Aboriginal and Torres Strait Islander people of Australia and the Maori of New Zealand. In the 1990s, conflict occurred in Fiji between the native Fijians and the descendants of Indians who came to Fiji to work on sugar plantations.

Exploring Australia and the Pacific

Pacific

→ Magellan (1519)

→ Roggeveen (1721)

→ Cook (1772)

Australia

→ Tasman (1642)

⇢ Tasman (1644)

→ Cook (1768)

→ Flinders (1802)

→ Burke and Wills (1860)

→ Stuart (1861)

Great events

The original inhabitants of Australia and the Pacific islands came from southeastern Asia thousands of years ago. European settlement on a large scale began only in the 1800s. The first settlers were convicts who worked in penal colonies, but they were soon followed by free settlers. The settlers took over Aboriginal lands and brought diseases that killed the people because they had no natural immunity. Within 200 years the Aboriginals were outnumbered by more than 50 to one. The British introduced sheep and cattle to their new colonies, discovered gold and developed industries and commerce. In the late 19th century Britain, France, Germany and the United States competed for control of the islands of the Pacific. However, since the 1960s, some twelve Pacific countries have won their independence. Today Australia and New Zealand are prosperous independent countries that trade all round the world, and especially with the United States and Japan.

Hawaii

MARSHALL ISLANDS

FIJI

Tahiti

AUSTRALIA

Easter Island

NEW ZEALAND

Important dates

40,000 Humans already settled in Australia

7000s Cultivators settled in New Guinea

5000s Sea levels rose and isolated Australia, New Zealand and Papua New Guinea

3000 Aboriginal rock paintings

1300s Melanesian settlers reached Fiji and Samoa

800s-900s New Zealand's North Island settled by Polynesian ancestors of the Maori

1519-21 Portuguese navigator Ferdinand Magellan became the first European to sail across the Pacific

1642-5 Abel Tasman sailed round Australia and visited New Zealand

1722 Dutch explorer Jacob Roggeveen discovered Easter Island and other islands in the South Pacific

1768 Captain James Cook began exploring the Pacific; he claimed New South Wales for Britain (1770)

1788 British established penal colony at Port Jackson (Sydney), governed by Arthur Phillip

1790s Australians set up whaling and sealing stations in New Zealand; European settlement began soon afterwards

1801-3 Matthew Flinders sailed round Australia and mapped the coast

1820s Wool industry established in Australia; free settlers encouraged

1840 Maori chiefs sign Treaty of Waitangi making New Zealand a British colony

40,000 BCE   1 CE

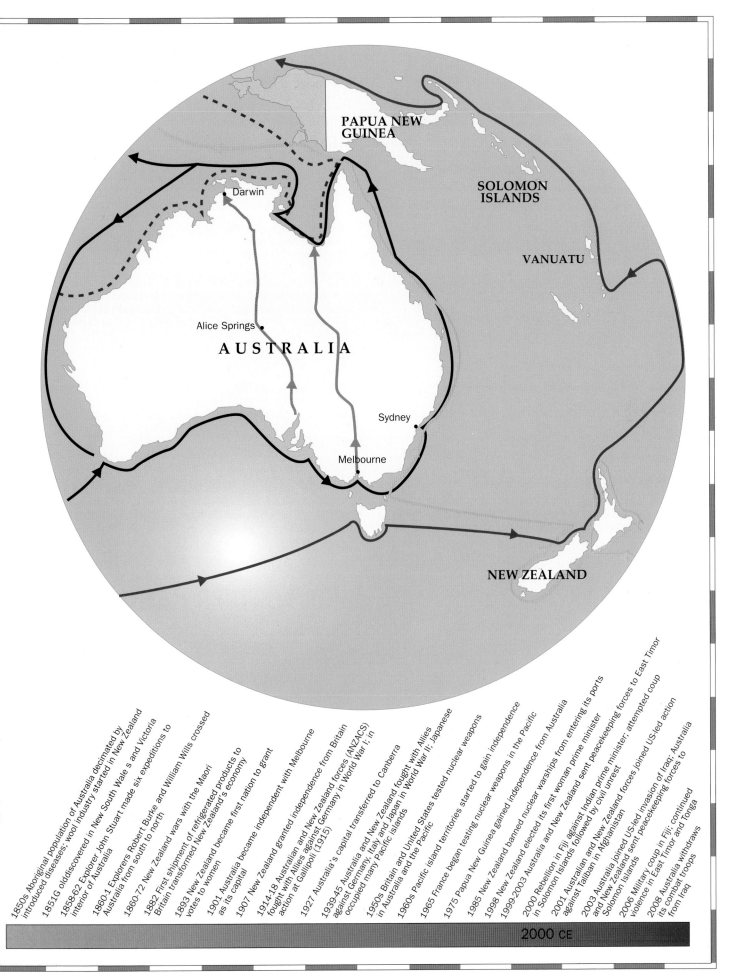

PAPUA NEW GUINEA

SOLOMON ISLANDS

VANUATU

Darwin

Alice Springs

AUSTRALIA

Sydney

Melbourne

NEW ZEALAND

1850s Aboriginal population of Australia decimated by introduced diseases; wool industry started in New Zealand

1851G olddiscovered in New South Wale s and Victoria

1858-62 Explorer John Stuart made six expeditions to interior of Australia

1860-1 Explorers Robert Burke and William Wills crossed Australia from south to north

1860-72 New Zealand wars with the Maori

1882 First shipment of refrigerated products to Britain transformed New Zealand's economy

1893 New Zealand became first nation to grant votes to women

1901 Australia became independent with Melbourne as its capital

1907 New Zealand granted independence from Britain

1914-18 Australian and New Zealand forces (ANZACS) fought with Allies against Germany in World War 1; in action at Gallipoli (1915)

1927 Australia's capital transferred to Canberra

1939-45 Australia and New Zealand fought with Allies against Germany, Italy and Japan in World War II; Japanese occupied many Pacific islands

1950s Britain and United States tested nuclear weapons in Australia and the Pacific

1960s Pacific island territories started to gain independence

1965 France began testing nuclear weapons in the Pacific

1975 Papua New Guinea gained independence from Australia

1985 New Zealand banned nuclear warships from entering its ports

1998 New Zealand elected its first woman prime minister

1999-2003 Australia and New Zealand sent peacekeeping forces to East Timor

2000 Rebellion in Fiji against Indian prime minister; attempted coup in Solomon Islands followed by civil unrest

2001 Australian and New Zealand forces joined US-led action against Taliban in Afghanistan

2003 Australia joined US-led invasion of Iraq; Australia and New Zealand sent peacekeeping forces to Solomon Islands

2006 Military coup in Fiji; continued violence in East Timor and Tonga

2008 Australia withdraws its combat troops from Iraq

2000 CE

Glossary

colonist A person who settles in a place that is not their native land.

convict A person who has been sentenced for committing a crime; a prisoner.

dense Crowded together, or highly concentrated.

dormant Being in a state of inactivity, or suspended animation.

endangered Being in danger of dying out or becoming extinct.

expedition A trip with an intended goal or purpose.

gemstone A stone that is precious or valuable.

hydroelectricity Electricity that has been generated by moving water, or hydropower.

immigrant A person who has moved to a different country, often to pursue work or labor.

indigenous The quality of being native to a place.

minority Belonging to a group that is smaller than the dominant group.

naturalist A person who studies nature

navigator An explorer that travels by boat or ship.

prosperous Wealthy or successful.

reef Coral ridges formed by billions of tiny organism. Coral reefs are found in the water offshore.

regatta A boat race.

sanctuary A safe-haven, or place of refuge.

tropical The tropics are located near the Earth's equator. The world tropical can refer to anything that characterizes this region, or can be used to describe anything situated in the tropics.

For More Information

Australian Permanent Mission to the United Nations
150 East 42nd Street
Level 33
New York, New York 10017
(212) 351-6600
Web site: http://www.australiaun.org/
An international organization that promotes peace, security, and economic development between nations, the United Nations has extended membership to nearly every sovereign nation on earth. Australia has been a UN member since 1945.

National Geographic Society
1145 17th Street N.W.
Washington, D.C. 20036-4688
(800) 647-5463
Web site: http://www.nationalgeographic.com/
This non-profit organization promotes science and education, and works to conserve both cultural and natural resources. Established in 1888, it is one of the world's largest educational non-profits.

New Zealand Embassy
37 Observatory Circle, NW
Washington D.C. 20008
(202) 328-4800
Web site: http://www.nzembassy.com/home.cfm?c=31
The New Zealand Embassy hands all of New Zealand's affairs with the United States.

WEB SITES

Due to the changing nature of Internet links, Rosen Publishing has developed an online list of Web sites related to the subject of this book. This site is updated regularly. Please use this link to access the list:

http://www.rosenlinks.com/atl/aust

For Further Reading

Arnold, Caroline. Uluru: *Australia's Aboriginal Heart*. New York, NY: Clarion Books, 2003.

Bantin, Erinn. *Australia the Land* (Land, Peoples, and Cultures). New York, NY: Crabtree Publishing Company, 2002.

Gillespie, Carol Ann. *New Zealand* (Modern World Nations). New York, NY: Chelsea House Publications, 2002.

Jacobs, Warren. *A Portrait of New Zealand*. New York, NY:

Rajendra, Vijeya and Sundran Rajendra. *Australia* (Cultures of the World). New York, NY: Benchmark Books, 2002.

De Roi, Tui and Mark Jacobs. *New Zealand: A Natural History*. Buffalo, NY: Firefly Books, 2006.

Smith, Ramsey W. *Myths and Legends of the Australian Aborigines*. Mineola, NY: Dover Publications, 2003.

Young, Abby. *Australia: A Primary Source Cultural Guide* (Primary Sources of World Cultures). New York: Rosen Publishing, 2005.

INDEX

A
Aboriginal art, 10, 44
Aboriginal people, 7, 10, 11, 37, 44, 45
Adelaide, 6, 12, 13, 36
Alice Springs, 10, 39
All Blacks, 25
American Samoa, 34
Antarctica, 8, 28, 40
Aorangi (Mount Cook), 22, 26
Apia, 34
apples, 14, 20, 21, 26
Arctic Ocean, 28
Argyle diamond mine, 8
atolls, 33
Auckland, 22, 24, 39
Auckland Regatta, 25
Australia, 4–5, 6–7, 22, 30, 36, 37, 38, 39, 40, 41, 42, 43, 44, 45
  New South Wales, 6, 13, 14, 16–17, 43, 44, 45
  Northern Territory, 10–11
  Queensland, 8, 13, 14–15, 43
  South Australia, 12–13
  Tasmania, 8, 20–21, 43
  Victoria, 13, 18–19, 43, 45
  Western Australia, 8–9, 13, 43
Australian Alps, 6, 17
Australian Capital Territory, 16
Australian Rules football, 18

B
Bairiki, 32
Banaba Island, 32
bananas, 14, 35
barley, 12, 14, 26
Bartle Frere, Mount, 14
Bass Strait, 20
bauxite, 8, 10, 42
Bay of Plenty, 22
Bering Strait, 28
Bligh, William, 35
Blue Mountains, 17
blue whale, 28
boating, 6, 15
Bogong, Mount, 18
boomerangs, 7
Bougainville, 30
Bounty, 35
breadfruit, 35
Brisbane, 6, 14, 15, 36, 39
Brisbane River, 15
Britain/England, 4, 6, 16, 20, 21, 30, 34, 44, 45

C
Campbell, Donald, 13
Canberra, 6, 16, 45
Canterbury Plains, 26, 27
carvings, 23
cattle ranching, 12, 14, 20, 24, 41, 44
Chinese gooseberries, 22
Christchurch, 27
Clutha River, 43
coal, 14, 18, 42, 43

coconuts, 31, 33, 35
convicts, 15, 44
Coober Pedy, 12
Cook, James, 4, 6, 22, 44
Cook Islands, 34
copper, 14, 20, 30, 42
copra, 31
coral/coral reefs, 14, 15, 28, 29, 32, 33
corn, 14
crocodiles, 11
crown-of-thorns starfish, 41

D
dairy farming, 8, 14, 19, 22, 24, 42
Darwin, 10, 11, 39
Darwin, Charles, 11
Derwent River, 21
desert, 8, 10, 12, 38, 41
diamonds, 8, 42
Dreaming, 37
Dutch, 6, 22

E
earthquakes, 41
Easter Island, 29, 34, 44
echidna, 17
Egmont, Mount, 24
Ellice Islands, 34
endangered species, 9, 11, 41
energy sources, 43
European settlement, 6, 15, 22, 40, 44
European Union, 21, 44
Eyre, Lake/Lake Eyre Salt Flats 12, 13

F
farming/agriculture, 4, 8, 9, 12, 14, 18, 19, 20, 24, 26, 27, 36, 40, 41, 42
Fiji, 5, 30, 31, 37, 43, 44, 45
Fiordland, 26
fishing, 31, 41
Flinders, Matthew, 10, 44
flowers, 35
flying fish, 29
Fongafale, 34
forests, 8, 20, 22, 25, 26, 33, 41
France, 30, 34, 44, 45
Fremantle, 9
French Polynesia, 34

G
Gairdner, Lake, 12
Germany, 44, 45
geysers, 5, 24
Gilbert Islands, 32
glaciers, 26
global warming, 40, 41
gold, 6, 8, 30, 44, 45
Gold Coast, 14
gold rushes, 6
grapes/wine making, 12, 18, 26
Great Barrier Reef, 14, 15, 41
Great Dividing Range, 6, 17
Griffin, Walter Burley, 16
gross domestic product, 43
Guam, 32

H
Hawaii, 4, 34
Hobart, 20, 21
Hobart Cup, 21
Honiara, 30
hurricanes, 39
hydroelectricity/hydroelectric dams, 19, 20, 25, 43

I
Indian Ocean, 8
Indonesia, 4, 30
International Date Line, 28
Ireland, 6
iron ore, 8, 20
Isa, Mount, 14

K
Kakadu National Park, 11
Kangaroo Island, 13
kangaroo paw, 8, 9
kangaroos, 4, 10, 13
kauri trees, 25
Kelly, Ned, 19
Kiribati, 5, 32, 40
kiwi fruit, 22
kiwis, 22
Koa, Mount, 34
koalas, 6, 14
Kosciuszko, Mount, 6, 16, 17
Kosciuszko National Park, 17

L
lead, 14
Likiep, 32

M
Mackinnon Pass, 27
Majuro, 32
Makarakomburu, Mount, 30
Malaysia, 28
manganese, 10, 42
manufacturing, 14, 15, 17, 18, 20, 22, 24, 42
Maori, 22, 23, 24, 26, 44, 45
Mariana Trench, 28
Marshall Islands, 5, 32, 40
marsupials, 4, 6, 9, 21
Mauga Silisli, 34
Meharry, Mount, 8
Melanesia, 28, 30–31, 32, 44
Melbourne, 4, 6, 18, 19, 36, 45
Melekeok, 32
Micronesia, 28, 32–33
Micronesia, Federated States of, 5, 32
Midway Island, 34
Milford Sound, 26
Milford Track, 27
minerals/mining, 8, 9, 10, 14, 20, 30, 33, 42
missionaries, 37
moa, 41
Murray River, 19

N
Nambung National Park, 8
national parks, 8, 11, 17

National Parks and Wildlife Service, 41
natural gas, 10, 18, 42, 43
Nauru, 5, 32, 33
New Caledonia, 30
Newcastle, 16
New Guinea, 30, 44
New Hebrides, 30
New South Wales, 6, 13, 14, 16–17, 43, 44, 45
New Zealand, 4–5, 22–23, 34, 36, 37, 38, 39, 40, 41, 42, 43, 44, 45
  North Island, 5, 22, 23, 24–25, 38, 39, 43, 44
  South Island, 26–27, 38, 43
Ngauruhoe, Mount, 24
Ngerchelchuus, Mount, 32
nickel, 8, 42
Niue, 5, 34
Niulakita, 34
Norfolk Island, 30
Northern Mariana Islands, 32
Northern Territory, 10–11
North Island, 5, 22, 23, 24–25, 38, 39, 43, 44
nuclear tests, 40, 41, 45
Nuku'alofa, 34
numbat, 8, 9, 41

O
Oceania, 4, 5
  climate and vegetation, 38–39
  ecology and environment, 40–41
  economy, 42–43
  main religions, 37
  politics and history, 44–45
  population, 4, 36–37
oil, 8, 10, 18, 30, 42
opals, 12
Ossa, Mount, 20
outrigger canoes, 29

P
Pacific islands, 4, 28–29, 36, 38, 40, 41, 42, 44, 45
  Melanesia, 30–31
  Micronesia, 32–33
  Polynesia, 34–35
Pacific Ocean, 4, 8, 15, 24, 28–29, 34, 40, 44
Palau, 5, 32, 33
Palikir, 32
palm oil, 31
Panama, 28
Papua New Guinea, 4, 18, 30, 31, 36, 37, 38, 41, 43, 44, 45
pearls/mother-of-pearl, 8
pears, 26
Perth, 6, 8, 9, 12, 36
phosphate rock, 33
pineapples, 14
Pinnacles Desert, 8
Pitcairn Islands Group, 34, 35
platypus, 16, 17

pollution, 40, 41
Polynesia, 28, 34–35, 41
Port Moresby, 30
Port-Vila, 30
potatoes, 19, 20, 26

Q
Queensland, 8, 13, 14–15, 43

R
radioactive contamination, 41
rainforests, 36, 38
road trains, 12
royal albatross, 27
Royal Flying Doctor Service, 7
Ruapehu, Mount, 23, 24
rugby, 18, 22, 25

S
sailing, 25
salt pans, 13
Samoa, 5, 34, 37, 41, 44
sea turtles, 34
sharks, 32
sheep, 8, 12, 14, 19, 20, 22, 27, 41, 44
shells, 34
silver, 14, 42
Snowy Mountains, 19, 43
solar energy plants, 43
Solomon Islands, 30, 31, 37, 38, 41, 43, 45
sorghum, 14
South Australia, 12–13
Southern Alps, 26
South Island, 26–27, 38, 43
spirit houses, 31
steam, 25
Stewart Island, 26
Stuart Highway, 12
Sturt, Charles, 10, 12
Sturt's desert pea, 12
Sturt's desert rose, 10
sugar cane, 14, 31
surfing, 15
Suva, 30
Swan River, 9
sweet potatoes, 35
Sydney, 6, 7, 16, 17, 19, 21, 36, 44
Sydney Harbour Bridge, 7
Sydney Opera House, 17

T
Tabwemasana, Mount, 30
taro, 35
Tasman, Abel, 20, 22, 44
Tasmania, 8, 20–21, 43
Tasmanian blue gum, 20
Tasmanian devil, 20, 21
Tasmanian wolf, 21, 41
thermal energy, 43
tin, 20, 42
Tokelau, 34, 40
Tomanivi, Mount, 30
Tonga, 5, 34, 35, 37, 45
Tongariro, Mount, 24
Torres Stait Islanders, 7, 44
Totolom, 32

tourism, 14, 17, 27, 30, 34
trekking/tramping, 27
tungsten, 42
Tuvalu, 5, 34, 37, 40
Twelve Apostles, 19

U
Uluru (Ayers Rock), 10, 11
United States, 4, 32, 34, 43, 44, 45
uranium, 10

V
Van Diemen's Land, 20
Vanuatu, 30, 31, 38, 41
Victoria, 13, 18–19, 43, 45
volcanoes, 5, 23, 24, 28, 29, 30, 33, 41, 43
votes for women, 23, 45

W
Waikato River, 25, 43
Waitaki River, 43
Wake Island, 32
Wallis & Futuna Islands, 34
waratah plants, 16
war chants, 22
washing machines, 17
Wave Rock, 9
Wellington, 22, 23, 24, 25
Western Australia, 8–9, 13, 43
Western Samoa, 34
whales/whaling, 21, 28, 44
wheat, 8, 12, 13, 14, 19, 26, 27, 42
Wilhelm, Mount, 30
Wollongong, 16
wood/paper products, 20, 21
Woodroffe, Mount, 12
wool, 19, 22, 27, 42, 44, 45

Y
Yaren, 32
Yarra River, 19

Z
Zeil, Mount, 10
zinc, 14, 20, 42

ABOUT THE AUTHORS

S. Joshua Comire is a writer living in Queens, New York.

Malcolm Porter is a leading cartographer for children's books. He has contributed to the *Times Atlas* and *Reader's Digest Atlas*, and has provided maps for leading educational and trade publishers. He drew the maps and designed the award-winning books *Atlas of the United States of America* and the *Collins Children's Atlas*.

Keith Lye is a best-selling author of geography titles for children of all ages. He is a distinguished contributor and consultant to major encyclopedias, including *Encyclopedia Britannica* and *World Book*.